Hunting
Lieutenant
Chadbourne

Jim W. Corder

Hunting
Lieutenant
Chadbourne

The University of Georgia Press
Athens and London

© 1993 by Jim W. Corder
All rights reserved
Published by the University of Georgia Press
Athens, Georgia 30602

Designed by Erin Kirk
Set in 10 on 13 Linotype Walbaum
by Tseng Information Systems, Inc.
Printed and bound by Thomson-Shore, Inc.
The paper in this book meets the guidelines for permanence and durability
of the Committee on Production Guidelines for Book Longevity of the
Council on Library Resources.

Printed in the United States of America
97 96 95 94 93   C   5 4 3 2 1

Library of Congress Cataloging in Publication Data
Corder, Jim W. (Jim Wayne), 1929–
    Hunting Lieutenant Chadbourne / Jim W. Corder.
      p.   cm.
    Includes bibliographical references.
    ISBN 0-8203-1503-6 (alk. paper)
    1. Chadbourne, Theodore Lincoln, 1822–1846.
    2. Mexican War, 1846–1848—Biography.
    3. Soldiers—Texas—Biography. I. Title.
    E403.1.C46C67   1993
    973.6′2′092—dc20
    [B]   92-19195
                                                                CIP

British Library Cataloging in Publication Data available

For Roberta
and for Kate,
who came later

Contents

viii

Contents

Acknowledgments

I am grateful to Katharine Waring and Robert E. Byrns of the Tom Green County Historical Society, who first gave me permission to use the Miles and Chadbourne papers. The papers are now housed in the library at Angelo State University in San Angelo, Texas. I appreciate the library's further permission. I am also grateful to Joyce Martindale, Interlibrary Loan Librarian at Texas Christian University, who was patient with me and both zealous and efficient in her searches.

Hunting
Lieutenant
Chadbourne

One

Perhaps I'll Never
Find Him

I carry a spiral notebook in my shirt pocket. It's bound at the top and measures three by five inches. I use it for telephone numbers and for lists of things I'm supposed to do or want to do and for names of books I want to find and for scribbles that may turn into something someday, or may not. The current notebook is nearly full and will soon go into a drawer with all the others, and I'll get a new one.

On one page of my notebook, the following note appears with the name Lieutenant Colonel W. G. Belknap:

> In the battle of the 9th, the 8th regiment lost, in Lieutenant Chad-bourne, a promising young officer, who fell in the manful discharge of duty.

Nothing else appears on the page. When I found the note, I didn't record the source. I don't remember why I didn't. I think I'll find the note again, and the longer document where it belongs. I think I scribbled it quickly while I was reading micro-filmed papers in the library. Colonel Belknap commanded the 8th Infantry Regiment in the Battle of Resaca de la Palma, on May 9, 1846. I think the note appears in his report following the battle to his commanding officer, General Zachary Taylor, and I think General Taylor incorporated Colonel Belknap's report into his own report to Washington. I think I'll find it again.

2   But I may not find Lieutenant Chadbourne. He was still
Perhaps   twenty-three when he died that day. Twenty-three years
I'll Never   doesn't give a fellow much time to compile records or build
Find Him   diaries or get into history books.

Two

Catching a Glimpse of Lieutenant Chadbourne

I had known for a long time that Fort Chadbourne once stood some miles to the southwest of Abilene, but I never paid any special attention until my daughter and her husband moved to San Angelo. Sometimes, when I went to see them, I took the route through Abilene and down. About two years ago, I noticed Lieutenant Chadbourne.

About halfway down the stretch of Highway 277 that takes you from Abilene to San Angelo, on a low bluff above the road on the left, there is a marker, just about all the evidence left of Fort Chadbourne.

The fort was established in 1852 by units of the 8th United States Infantry and was also a station on the Butterfield stage and mail line. The state of Texas took it over as the Civil War was beginning. United States troops occupied it for a short while after the war, but then Chadbourne gave way to the new Fort Concho down the road in what would be San Angelo. Concho had better water, and it put troops nearer to where they were then needed. Now the marker is about all that remains of Fort Chadbourne.

But during the 1850s, life was active enough there. A band of Comanches stole a small herd of horses while passengers on the Butterfield stage were watching. A Captain Van Buren was

killed nearby in 1854. Comanches took two military mail carriers, tied them to a tree, and burned them. Rupert N. Richardson tells of a soldier "who after an attack by Indians managed
to get into the post, even though he had fourteen arrows in him
and bristled like a porcupine. A doctor removed the arrows, and
within two weeks the soldier was walking around." Richardson
also tells of nonviolent times:

> Happily not all the relations between the races at Fort Chadbourne
> had to do with tomahawk and rifle. When the wife of Dr. Ebenezer
> Swift, the post surgeon, gave birth to a baby boy the squaws formed
> a line to see the white baby. "Chiquito Medico," Little Doctor, they
> called the child. (Many Texas Comanches spoke a little Spanish.)
> In *Our Wild Indians*, Colonel Richard M. Dodge, who knew the Old
> West from experience, attaches to Fort Chadbourne a tale told all
> along the Great Plains frontier. Indians were fond of horse-racing
> and gambling and not infrequently officers and troops at frontier
> posts would match them. Mu-la-que-top, a Comanche, matched
> with an officer at the fort a race in which the Indian's sheep-like
> pony bested a fine Kentucky mare belonging to the officer. The red
> man added insult to financial injury by riding the last fifty yards of
> the race head to tail, beckoning the rider of the mare to come on.

Fort Chadbourne was named for Lieutenant Theodore L.
Chadbourne. He was born in Eastport, Maine, on August 2,
1822. He was graduated from West Point on July 1, 1843,

commissioned brevet second lieutenant, and assigned to the
infantry at Fort Niagara, where he spent about two years.
Promoted to second lieutenant, he was reassigned to the 8th
Infantry Regiment and transferred to the Military Occupation
of Texas, where he joined Zachary Taylor's army not too far
from Brownsville. He fought in the Battle of Palo Alto on
May 8, 1846. On the next day, May 9, 1846, he was killed
in the Battle of Resaca de la Palma. Otherwise, I can't find
him; nothing tells me much. A register of West Point graduates shows that Theodore Lincoln Chadbourne was fifteenth
in the class of 1843. When he died at Resaca de la Palma he
was still twenty-three. Ulysses S. Grant was twenty-first in the
same class. Otherwise, I can't find him; nothing tells me much.
He didn't make it into the *Dictionary of American Biography*.

On down the road, in San Angelo, there are other traces. One
of the main streets in the city is Chadbourne Street. Maybe
it, too, was named for him. Maybe it was named, instead, for
the fort. Maybe it's the old road leading back up to Fort Chadbourne.

His tunic hangs in a glass case in the museum that is in
the headquarters building of old Fort Concho. A white strap
hangs down from the right shoulder and across the chest to the
waist on the left, where his sword is. In the center of the strap,
over the heart, there is a neat bullet hole. He was young, still
twenty-three, and a long way from home, though younger men
have died in farther places.

I have stood before that case and wondered how it was with
him. I have wondered how and when his family came to know
that he had been killed. Friends in the history department
where I teach tell me that they can only make guesses about
how the word got back home. Perhaps, one guesses, by courier
to a boat waiting at the mouth of the Rio Grande, then to New
Orleans to a mail boat there and on to New York, then by slow
post to Maine, or wherever his parents were by then. Another
colleague suggests that messages maybe had to go by courier
all the way to Galveston, then by boat to New Orleans, or direct
to New York. They say it must have taken two months, maybe
a little less, maybe a lot longer.

What's it like, I have wondered, to learn that you have hov-
ered in anxiety over a young man's welfare, worried about him,

held him in your mind, prayed for him, long after he was dead? It must be unspeakably hard for a family.

But harder, I expect, to be a young man, probably hot that May 9, 1846, maybe dirty, maybe scared, certainly dead, at twenty-three.

Three

But Sometimes When
I Look, I Don't See

But that—what I've just written—was two years or so ago, and it's wrong in some important ways.

I relied too much on my own memory, on assumptions and chance testimony. I had wondered if Lieutenant Chadbourne's parents were still in Eastport, Maine, when he was killed, assuming too quickly that folks don't stay still. Apparently they were, and at least some members of his family were still there generations later. I had wondered how long it took for them to learn of his death and guessed from the guesses of others that it might have been two months or longer. It wasn't. Reports of the Battle of Resaca de la Palma and its casualties reached Washington, D.C., on May 23, just two weeks after the battle, and stories appeared in eastern newspapers on May 26. I still don't know how word got there so soon.

I relied too much on my own memory untested, remarking that a historical marker is "just about all the evidence left of Fort Chadbourne." That's not true. If I had paid attention and looked more closely, I would have known. Ray Miller's *Texas Forts* has a picture of Fort Chadbourne's ruins. "The site," Miller reports, "is private property and the stone buildings are ruins." Miller's *Eyes of Texas Travel Guide* (Hill Country/ Permian Basin Edition) says that "the ruins of old Fort Chadbourne are in the northeastern corner of the County [Coke

County], just off U.S. 277, about 12 miles north of Bronte. Only a few rock walls remain at the site. Nothing much is left, either, of the town of Fort Chadbourne that grew up outside the military post in the early days." The same book shows a different picture of the ruins. In the caption below the picture, this notice occurs: "This is private property and tourists are not welcome." Charles M. Robinson's *Frontier Forts of Texas*, with yet a different picture of the ruins, has this account:

> Today, the most visible ruins are those of the two stone barracks and two of the officers' houses. Most of the other buildings exist only as half-buried foundations. The post is located on Chadbourne Ranch, about 100 yards from the main office. While I received total cooperation from the ranch management during my visit, it should be brought out that Chadbourne is a working cattle ranch and not a tourist attraction. The serious student would do best to call the ranch from Bronte, to determine whether it is convenient to visit. The public can read the Fort Chadbourne historical marker on a rise from U.S. 277 overlooking the post, and visit the nearby cemetery.

A fuller account, with still other pictures, occurs in Jessie Newton Yarbrough's *History of Coke County*, but I'll save what she says until later.

And there's worse, in my mind: I relied too much on my own observation, especially on my memory of my own observation. I said that his tunic hangs in a glass case with his sword and sword belt. The sword is there, and the sword belt, with the neat bullet hole in the strap that comes down from the right shoulder to the left waist. The tunic is not there. I glanced and trusted my glance, and then trusted my memory of the glance. Over the headless bust that holds the sword belt there is no tunic, only anonymous dark blue cloth. I went back later and saw that I had not seen.

Four

Memory and History

I have wondered why I trusted my memory to tell me that his tunic, not just his sword belt, was there in the case in the head-quarters building at Fort Concho. Why was I astonished when I found that I was wrong? Why was I so late to learn the falli-bility of my memory? I had known all along that some people, places, events, things didn't get into my memory, but if things did get into my memory, I thought they were there accurately.

But that's never actually been the case. People, places, events, things never did "get into" my memory, as though into a file. I created them and located them to fit whatever story I was telling of myself. But surely I know what I saw? Sometimes surely.

But sometimes I didn't see what I thought I saw, and then in the telling misremembered both what I thought I saw and whatever I may have seen. Sometimes I saw what I didn't know I saw and so had no way of telling. I have known for a long time that memory fails, but I guess I knew that only conventionally, not tellingly, and I guess I didn't know that memory would fail when I told of sacred moments and places.

I had told stories about the Texas Theater in Jayton for years, about seeing parts of the Zorro serial there, about the time when Jesse James honest-to-God showed up about fifty-five years after he got away from the dirty little coward who tried to kill him, about momentarily losing one of two nickels—maybe the last in the house—that would get me in, and about the instant ache that came until I found it, and about the sickness that pulses in me even now when I think about it. But a couple of years ago, I finally found copies of the *Jayton Chronicle* from the 1930s and discovered that it wasn't the Texas Theater after all. For a while it was the Palace, then it was the Kent, then it was the Texan, but it was never the Texas. Astonishing, if only to me.

How could I not have remembered some things? The *Jayton Chronicle* for December 8, 1938, says that sweet, red-haired Peggy Sue Robinson and I had the leading roles in the third-grade Christmas play that was presented before the whole school. How could I have forgotten? I loved her deeply, though from afar. The paper says it happened. I have no recollection of the event at all. I'd swear to God I didn't do it.

And how did I get it wrong about the train ride? For years I had told my children, friends, and passing strangers about my first train ride (and my only train ride until long after I was grown) from Gilpin, the post office and service station near Grandpa Durham's farm, all the twenty miles home to Jayton. Outfitted with a sack of Grandma's tea cakes, I rode home, the only passenger in the caboose, feeling the soft leather of the seat, touching the gleaming wood. But it wasn't my first or only train ride. Under "School News" the *Chronicle* for October 21, 1937, has a short, two-paragraph report of the second grade's class trip, a train ride up to Girard, some ten miles away. The name of the author of the report is printed right there in the newspaper. It's my name. What I saw, I often saw wrong and then misremembered, or forgot altogether. Most things I didn't see at all.

When memory fails, do I fail? Memory is the tale we tell of ourselves; it is the selves we keep constructing in our continuing narratives. We can't deny memory, can we, without feeling the cold on our backs, the shivers in our shoulders? Have I told myself wrongly, constructed the wrong self? If I didn't see what I thought I saw and then misremembered it all in the telling, have I lost my existence? If I got it all wrong in memory, did I get myself wrong? Am I not who I was?

Am I alone? Does everyone else remember well and trust the remembering? Does everyone else get it right the first time

and remember accurately forever after? We often talk to each
other as if we trust memory, as if we always know indubitably
which right self right memory tells.

When Tobias Wolff's book *This Boy's Life* was published,
I judge that some reviewers didn't know whether to call it a
novel or a memoir. Joel Conarroe, who reviewed the book in
the *New York Times Book Review* (January 15, 1989), takes the
work as "straight autobiography," though he adds later, "there
may or may not be convincing reasons to believe everything
Mr. Wolff tells us." As he concludes, Conarroe remarks that
"whatever liberties Mr. Wolff may have taken with the facts of
his boyhood in their memoir (and he admits in the preface that
memory has its own tale to tell), I found myself convinced by
the sharply etched details and more than willing to suspend
any disbelief." At a time when literary critics and theorists have
told us frequently and compellingly that writers are bereft of
their texts, which already belong to interpreting readers, it's
strange and a little confusing that reviewers would surrender
themselves in favor of whatever truth—whether truth as fiction or truth as memoir—an author is willing to give. But then,
whatever is given doesn't have to be truth, does it? If whatever is given might be either novel or memoir, then what some
call truth is not an issue. Whatever is given doesn't have to
measure itself—nor do we have to measure it—against what
might have happened somewhere sometime. If neither author
nor reader but text is our focus, then textuality is the issue and
there need be no coincidence between whatever is given as
text and whatever might be another reality. Whatever mani-
fests itself as text—that is, whatever has issued from memory
but is now text, not memory—is sufficient. Memory is already
sanctified and sufficient, even when it very plainly is not.

How can you know when you've got it right? Will memory
ever catch just what happened and bring it untransformed into
the present?

Not so long ago, I read William Manchester's "Bloodiest
Battle of All" (*New York Times Magazine*, June 14, 1987), a
moving account of his personal experience at Okinawa, "the
last and bloodiest battle of the Pacific war." When we count
Americans, Japanese, and Okinawans, Manchester reports,

more than 200,000 perished in the 82-day struggle—twice the number of Japanese lost at Hiroshima and more American blood than had been shed at Gettysburg. My own regiment—I was a sergeant in the 19th Marines—lost more than 80 percent of the men who landed on April 1, 1945. Before the battle was over, both the Japanese and American commanding generals lay in shallow graves.

The article is his account of "what I knew and when I knew it." Meditating for a moment on Memorial Day parades, Manchester asks,

> But what of those who *do* remain faithful to patriotic holidays? What are they commemorating? Very rarely are they honoring what actually happened, because only a handful know, and it's not their favorite topic of conversation. In World War II, 16 million Americans entered the armed forces. Of these, fewer than a million saw action. Logistically, it took 19 men to back up one man in combat. All who wore uniforms are called veterans, but more than 90 percent of them are as uninformed about the killing zones as those on the home front.

Only a handful know what actually happened. But how do you know when you know? How do you know that what you have in your memory is what happened?

I don't doubt the reality Manchester carries in his head, or its heaviness for him. He was wounded twice on Okinawa, the second time gravely, in my stead. But I need to know how you know that you've got it right. Telling of the deadly combat before the marines captured Sugar Loaf Hill, Manchester reports: "During those 10 days I ate half a candy bar. I couldn't keep anything down." How can I doubt him? I do doubt him. Every particular is blessed; none is insignificant. How do you know when you know? Can we trust memory? We mostly do. But might it have been two-thirds of a candy bar, or one-third? Might it have been eight and a half days or nine days, or even just a long time? Does memory work accurately for some, and not for others? We trust memory. Is it always right, an accurate rendering not of our past but of the narrative we're always creating for ourselves? Is it always wrong? I can almost catch how I felt when I climbed the windmill at Grandpa Durham's farm, but I can't catch how he felt when he paused to look out across the fields. Was Manchester's half of a candy bar the reality that was, the reality that others knew? How do you know when

you know?

I can't shake myself loose from the question, but others seem
to manage better. In his essay "In the Whirl and Muddle of
War," Samuel Hynes writes about war memories, published
and unpublished, and suggests that some men who have fought

> have had a deep need to record what they saw and felt. Not for *us*,
> I think, but for themselves, to say like the ubiquitous Kilroy, *I was
> there*. And perhaps also to try to order the meaningless incoherence
> that a war seems to be to those who fight, not misrepresenting the
> disorder but putting down plainly what happened and so, perhaps,
> finding themselves.

Putting down plainly what happened. How in the hell can you
do that? Some apparently can. In the instance of war memoirs, Hynes suggests, it sometimes requires a wait of years,
for understanding comes slowly, "and imagination must wait
upon memory to reveal itself." But what if memory is wrong?
What if imagination and memory are in each other or create
each other? Then how do you put down plainly what happened? As he thinks about older men writing memoirs of the
wars they fought when young, Hynes remembers Manchester's
Goodbye Darkness, published some years before the essay I
mentioned above:

> It is their older selves, the selves on the other side of those deep
> changes, who write the memoirs. They look back on themselves
> when young, when innocent, as though on another life, and the
> questions they ask of memory are different from those that a young
> man asks. The usual narrative questions are posed: What happened
> *there*? What happened *then*? But behind them are deeper questions:
> Who was I then? What happened to me? Who did I become? Cour-
> age is no longer the challenge; that question has been answered.
> Truth of being is what matters now. So William Manchester, after
> 30 years of *not* remembering his life as a young marine, returned
> to the islands to rediscover it and wrote a fine book about it. "This,
> then," he writes at the end of his narrative, "was the life I knew,
> where death sought me, during which I was transformed from a
> cheeky youth to a troubled man who, for over thirty years, repressed
> what he could not bear to remember." By then he *had* remembered,
> and had come to terms with his memories.

Except. Except. I don't think people, places, and events are stored intact in memory, and I don't think memory emerges intact later in the present.

But we talk and behave as if our perceptions correspond to some reality, as if this reality is then stored away, as if memory could then retrieve it, presenting the past. Sometimes we forget, to be sure, but when we remember, we get it right, or so we seem to believe—or act as if we believe—for we get through most days on the strength of memories that we take to be accurate, whether or not they are.

Sometimes we fill empty places in our narrative of ourselves by stretching the memory of unique events or occasional events so that they become regular events. Who can talk long about childhood or youth without a sentence that begins, "We used to . . ."? *Used to* is often the signal of one telling event, or a few such repeated events, but our sentences convert the special but infrequent into the special and routine. Early in *An American Childhood*, Annie Dillard tells about the time her father quit his job:

> I was sorry he'd be leaving the Manufacturer's Building down-town. From his office on the fourteenth floor, he often saw suicides, which he reported at dinner. The suicides grieved him, but they thrilled us kids. . . . People jumped from the Sixth Street bridge into the Allegheny River. Because the bridge was low, they shin-nied all the way up the steel suspension cables to the bridge towers before they jumped. Father saw them from his desk in silhouette, far away. . . . Pittsburgh was a cheerful town, and had far fewer suicides than most other cities its size. Yet people jumped so often that Father and his colleagues on the fourteenth floor had a betting pool going. They guessed the date and time of day the next jumper would appear.

Did suicides and threatened suicides occur as frequently as he remembered and reported? Did they occur as frequently as she, in her turn, remembered and reported? I don't know; I doubt it. The files of the *Pittsburgh Press* in the Carnegie Library in Pittsburgh might help me to know for sure, but I'm not much interested in checking. I take her word in the matter.

Though I continue to question memory—hers, mine, all

others'; and I'm not, of course, alone. When he made his leap

to death, had Primo Levi come to know that if memory doesn't somehow work, as it somehow doesn't, life is gone? An advertisement for his book *The Drowned and the Saved* in the *New York Review of Books* cites partial responses of various reviewers. According to the *Chicago Sun-Times Book Week*, the book "reveals the fallibility of memory, the tendency of both victims and oppressors to revise their experiences into simpler, more easily explainable forms." Alexander Stille, in the *New York Times Book Review*, remarks that "by the end of his life Levi had become increasingly convinced that the lessons of the Holocaust were destined to be lost as it took a place among routine atrocities of history." Richard Eder, in the *Los Angeles Times Book Review*, says, "After having told us what happened, Levi is now asking: What really happened? He relied upon memory and now he questions the very act of remembering."

(Do you inquire why I cite reviews rather than the books reviewed? Because I'm interested in how people react to the recorded memories of other people.)

And we should question memory: it's never accurate. The brain does not simply receive and store information about people, places, and events; it is a creator of memory. Freud, for example, seems to have believed that memories are part of a fixed record, inaccuracies being accounted for by later *rearrangements* and *retranscriptions*. Now, however, some suppose, as Israel Rosenfield writes, "that our capacity to remember is not for some specific recall of an image stored somewhere in our brain. . . . One reason why the search for memory molecules and specific information storage zones in the brain has so far been fruitless may be that they are just not there." Gerald Edelman's theory of neuronal group selection suggests that brain function depends not on localized functions and fixed memories but on the context and history of events in the world, which change, and on the context and history of networked brain units, which also change. As Rosenfield says, each person's "perceptions are to some degree creations and his or her memories are part of an ongoing process of imagination. A mental life cannot be attributed to molecules. Human intelligence is not just knowing more, but reworking, recategorizing, and thus generalizing information in new and surprising ways." We make what we remember. Claire Tomalin, in a review of Muriel Spark's *Mary Shelley: A Biography*, notes that Shelley "created an illusion about himself which he left as a heavy legacy to Mary; it had the effect of falsifying her memory of their life together and setting her perpetually at odds with reality. Even while he lived, the rift between his ideal existence and their actual experience was burdensome to Mary."

(And if memory is inaccurate, what shall we do about the novels, poems, plays, and essays we read? While we've long since become sophisticated enough in our reading to know about unreliable narrators in novels, what does it mean when we reckon that *all* speakers are unreliable? We have to rely on their memories, and their memories are inaccurate.)

Perhaps we always have to act as if we could remember, to live as memory teaches us, to believe that we remember. If we don't remember the past and imagine the future, our energy fails. We have to act and live and believe all the more because memory does fail. We are not so different, perhaps, from novelists, as Bruce Duffy identifies them: "What most distinguishes the novelist is a singular quality of memory, a memory in which the imaginative impulse is stronger than that of fidelity"—the imaginative impulse, we might say, or the self-creating impulse. At any rate, we trust memory, or I guess most do. Are all those others right? Are their memories accurate? A combat veteran interviewed in Studs Terkel's *Good War* says, "I was in combat for six weeks, but I can remember every hour, every minute of the whole 42 days." I do not doubt that he believes it is so, though it isn't.

And why shouldn't we trust memory? As it is wrong, memory is also right. It has its own order, structure, sense. First we trust our perceptions, and then we trust our recollection of what we think our perceptions were. If perceptions and memories turn out to be inaccurate, we have not lied: we have constructed a new version of ourselves. We probably shouldn't expect others to submit easily to *our* facts, or what we take to be facts. They will oftener than not live their lives as their memories have taught them. Martin Filler, writing about Frank Lloyd Wright's "largely unreliable" autobiography, claims its peculiar truth:

First published in 1932, with a substantially revised edition in 1943

(and a corrected version of that published posthumously in 1977), "An Autobiography" has manifold distortions, fantasies, prevarications and chronological inaccuracies that have kept scholars busy proving why this or that episode could not possibly have occurred in the way Wright described it. Yet the book remains by far the most vivid and, in some essential sense, the most veracious evocation of its chimerical author.

And we should not be surprised if, for example, Kurt Waldheim survives politically. While we may agree entirely with Shirley Hazzard, in a review of a book about Waldheim, that "from the chronicle of Mr. Waldheim's war years in the Balkans, the reader emerges incredulous that any man could deny such experience," we also know that we are always in some sense self-made. In his mind, he is *other*; not what all those people say but self, self-created, fit. Each of us accumulates evidence and insight, ignores some of it, fails to find other pieces, or chooses not to look. Each of us creates the history he or she can enjoy, or tolerate, or look at and put safely away. Each of us forms a conception of the world: its institutions, its public, private, wide, or local histories, and of ourselves among them all. We aren't always very good at it. Sometimes we don't see enough. Sometimes we find enough and see enough and still tell it wrong. Sometimes we fail to judge; sometimes we judge dogmatically, even ignorantly, obeying only the standards we have already established. We see only what our eyes will let us see at a given time, but eventually we make a history for ourselves that we can tolerate or at least not have to think about too much—or else we don't and have to be put away. Every so often, one of us will see something he or she or we have not seen before, and then we have to remake our various histories, revising ourselves. Some, however, will never see or hear any history but the one they've already made. To others, that may seem at least unthinking, perhaps evil, but the person who behaves so will probably not agree. That person, like Waldheim, will be in his or her memory, inside a history where it's possible to live.

Memory is always wrong and right. It's the text we make as we can, the fiction, memoir, or history that we call life, all made texts that can be revised, though we are slow to learn revision.

Revision is seeing again. Can we ever get situated to see, or to resee, what may have happened, who may have been, where we might have lived? Can we ever speak truthfully and openly if memory is always wrong? Memory is always wrong if we expect it to correspond exactly to a reality out there. If we ever caught some reality out there, we must have lost it if we can face what Daniel J. Boorstin describes: "how partial is the remaining evidence of the whole human past, how casual and how accidental is the survival of its relics." Seeing an old, filled-in trench near Rheims, its character still recognizable from World War I, remembering the soldierly phantasms who fought there, Louis Simpson writes:

> The greater part of life has not been expressed. The simple and illiterate, those who sustain the labor and pain of existence, those who carry out the orders, are never themselves heard. History neglects to mention them; most art admits little of their existence. Yet on the hill near Rheims, and at other times in my life, I have seen for a moment into the depth of this life, and it has given me an instinctive distrust of expressed ideas. If most of man's life has passed into silence, is not truth silent? . . . The very stars in their silence, and God, if he exists, by his absence, sympathize with what has not been spoken.

But yes, memory is right. Our constructions are what we have. Yes. No.

Memory is our atonement.

Then if memory fails, atonement is impossible.

Except we remember the possibility of revision, though we can't always revise; sometimes cannot, sometimes will not.

We trust ourselves, trust memory, trust what we call study to get history right. Often we're wrong. Maybe mostly.

I thought I'd be the first to hunt Lieutenant Chadbourne. I wasn't.

I thought I knew that his tunic was there in the case with his sword belt at Fort Concho. I was wrong.

I thought that Fort Chadbourne was right above the highway that runs from Abilene to San Angelo. I was wrong. Only a historical marker is there. The ruins of the fort are some distance away. Then I was to learn that those who had located the fort weren't altogether right either. Fort Chadbourne is a little farther away than any of us knew and as hard to locate as Lieutenant Chadbourne.

Eventually I was to learn again from Susan Miles of San Angelo, herself long dead, that I could not, need not, rely alone on my own memory.

Five

Looking Again

The little piece I had written about him earlier, which I've already reproduced here, kept Lieutenant Chadbourne in my mind. The piece was published elsewhere as if it were somehow true. In some ways it is, but not in all. I was wrong about the tunic. I was wrong about how long it might have taken his family to learn about his death. I had not, as I thought, seen the location of the fort named for him.

I began to wonder what else I had learned wrong, or hadn't learned at all.

But I didn't start to look for him, except casually and intermittently. Then a friend, an officer of the Army ROTC staff on the campus where I teach, told me about the *Cullum Register of Graduates and Former Cadets* and loaned me the ROTC office copy. He was on page 237:

> 1181 Theodore Lincoln Chadbourne
> B-ME: A-Lge: Inf: Kld Resaca de la Palma 9 May 46
> 2 LT a-23.

Cadet graduate number 1181, counting from the academy's first graduating class; he was born in Maine but appointed at large. He was a twenty-three-year-old second lieutenant when he was killed on May 9, 1846.

I had to shove him aside while I finished some other pieces of work, but he has been in my mind since I saw the entry, and I have been looking for him.

Six

Death Has Undone So Many: A Little Meditation on Parades and Memorials and on Mortality Records

After a while, I began to learn a little about Lieutenant Chadbourne. Not much at first because I veered off to other names that usurped my interest as I began to think that we should remember and say them.

I don't think I always knew that. Sometimes I think that I don't know it fully yet, but am only beginning to learn. Much inclined toward pacifism and sometimes generally and unre-flectively prejudicial toward the military, I am slow to learn, but we should remember the names. If I can't, someone should say the names, of friends and enemies, of those we never heard about or knew.

I began to learn their names when I was looking elsewhere and thinking about other things. I was trying to learn about Second Lieutenant Theodore Lincoln Chadbourne, though he wasn't easy to find. When I did find information beyond what I already knew about him—those brief lines in the *Register*—other information on the same page caught me and I couldn't get away. Images and ideas tumbled in my mind, sometimes

at first disjointed but finally maybe connected a little. Telling
how that can be requires going, for a moment, the long way
around.

When I came home from the army at the end of November
1952, there were no parades. I don't know about the others,
but I did not want parades, had no need of parades, had not
earned parades. My brother and his kind, my friend and his
kind had already warranted parades. Some of them died in
strange places.

My brother and his kind, mostly young men at least five
years older than I, served with more than 16 million others
in World War II, what some call the last just and knowable
war. Of those 16 million, more than 400,000 died, 292,000 or
more in "battle deaths," 115,000 in "other deaths." They were,
I thought, better than we younger folk, and they died in strange
places—at Kasserine Pass, or Salerno, or on the Anzio beach-
head, or on Guadalcanal, or near Midway, or at Iwo Jima, or
Omaha Beach, or over Ploesti, or by Remagen Bridge, or elsewhere. Of 16 million, more than 400,000 died.

My friend and his kind, mostly young men about my age,
served in Korea. Of more than 5 million in the services at the
time, some 54,000 died: 33,000 or so in "battle deaths," 20,000
or more in "other deaths." They went into peril, and I did not,
through the fortunes of war, the vagaries of the draft board, the
chance of time, and the needs of units when we were inducted
or called up from the reserves. Some of them died in strange
places—near Seoul, by the Inchon Reservoir, elsewhere. Of
more than 5 million, some 54,000 died, and there were no
parades, though parades were warranted.

I lived for two years in the army without peril, first at Fort
Hood, Texas, then at Coleman Barracks outside Mannheim,
Germany, though diverse officers expected me to be alert, as if
in peril. Others died while I was safe.

I did not think too much on such things until years later,
when, for a moment sullen, I came to wonder why veterans
of Vietnam raised such commotions, asked so loudly to be
noticed. I know they hurt. During the Vietnam years, more
than 8 million men and women served in the military. "Battle
deaths" came to way beyond 47,000; "other deaths" came to
way beyond 10,000. Of 8 million, on past 58,000 died. I know

those who came back hurt for those who didn't, and for them-

selves—and yet I resisted. I saw them from time to time on
TV—and I resisted. I remembered that nearly as many died
during four Korea years as died during ten Vietnam years, and
there were no parades, no memorials. I saw them from time
to time on TV, and I resisted: even though I took no delight in
military protocol, when I saw them demonstrating publicly in
combat fatigues or whatever, I heard myself muttering, "Class
A uniforms, please, goddam it, and dress that line." They forgot, I thought, that coming home from Vietnam was not the
same as coming home, say, from Europe when that part of
World War II was over. Then, whole units, or whatever was left
of them, came home together, in troopship after troopship, and
there were occasions and people enough for parades, a world's
deep sigh of gladness for memorials. By contrast, most of those
who returned from Korea and from Vietnam returned by rota-
tion, typically in smaller groups or individually, and there were
no parades. But the veterans of Vietnam got their time on TV
and their memorial. My friend and his kind who were in Korea
didn't. They were of a quieter generation, and there were no
parades.

I was sullen for a while before I came to know again that
those who came back from Vietnam hurt for those who didn't
and for themselves, and it was just and right. I reflected with
some horror on my own resistance and came to cringe at what
seemed my own resentment: Let no one, I finally was able
to think, begrudge commemoration, or withhold it long, for
young men who die, whether friend or enemy or someone we
never heard about or knew. We have all too often not noticed at
all or waited far too long. It required forty years before French
and German veterans of Verdun could come together there and
greet each other, grieve for the half million dead, and sing "Ich
hatte einen Kameraden." It required forty years before German
and American veterans of the fighting around the Remagen
Bridge could come together there, greet each other, and grieve
together for those who died. After forty years there were no
parades, but they took notice of each other. Often, we take no
notice.

And young men shouldn't have to ask for notice. We should
remember and give notice. It's hard to ask for notice, as no

doubt the Vietnam veterans have found, hard to claim that
any group has given the most, or even enough. Someone has
always died sooner and harder; some group has always lost
more. That's the way it is with others: I lived safely while others
died; they do that.

And that brings me to the names I began with. When I first
began to find them, though I was looking in another direction
and thinking about other things, I was caught and couldn't
get loose.

I had been looking to learn about Second Lieutenant Theodore Lincoln Chadbourne and not finding much. He didn't
live long enough to make it into many history books, though
he did have Fort Chadbourne as his marker. His sword is in
the Fort Concho museum, and his sword strap, with the neat
bullet hole. I wanted to know more about him but found little.

Then a friend suggested that I try the *Cullum Memorial
Edition of the Register of Graduates and Former Cadets of the
United States Military Academy, 1802–1970.* I did, and there he
was, on page 237, fifteenth in the class of 1843. He was born in
August 1822 and died in May 1846, still twenty-three, killed in
the Battle of Resaca de la Palma. I learned elsewhere later that
his parents lived in Eastport, Maine, and apparently did so for
long years after—a photograph in the Fort Concho museum
shows the Chadbourne family home in Eastport at around the
turn of the century, and some family at least was still there. I
wondered how long it would take for them to find out in Eastport that their son had died at Resaca de la Palma. I found no
certain answer, but that's all right: that's what parents think
about, I suppose, not what young men think about when they
go into battle.

But on the same page where I found him, other items caught
my attention. U. S. Grant was in the same class, though lower
in academic standing. Since I'm not a professional historian, I
felt no need to shun the "what if" school of history and found
myself wondering what would have happened if these young
men hadn't died. Would they have changed the world? Did
lesser men become leaders because they were gone? Would we
have been better? Worse?

I began to look, casually at first, at other classes during the
years before the Civil War. Before long, I was caught up in
the record, not in the "what if" school of thought. As I looked

through those pages of the *Register*, I began to see more and
more losses. I stopped and started over, trying this time to be a
little more systematic.

I wanted to start early enough to include Lieutenant Chadbourne. If I started looking at the record for the 1842 graduating class, that would give me records for twenty years, a nice
round number, if I stopped with the graduates of 1861.

In that period of twenty years, 856 young men are listed.
Of that group, 62, or 7 percent, were retired early as disabled,
mustered out with wounds, and the like, all young. Of the 856,
162, or about 19 percent, went into the service of the Confederacy, but their records continue in the *Register*. Of the 856, 284,
or 33 percent, died young. It's not a large group by comparison
with the figures from later wars, but the losses were uncommon. In those twenty years, and immediately thereafter in the
Civil War, there were many occasions for dying, and death un-
did about a third of that particular group of young men. What
did we lose? Too many young men.

They were, to be sure, in a high-risk profession, but perhaps
we asked more than we ought of them, and perhaps they gave
too little care to themselves. Perhaps, as Evan S. Connell suggests, none of us ever really learns to learn from experience. In
Son of the Morning Star, Connell tells of the deaths of Major
Elliott and his group in Custer's fight on the Washita River:

> When Elliott rode off in pursuit of the escaping Cheyennes he
> turned in the saddle, waved to Lt. Owen Hale, and delivered a
> line which sounds theatrical: "Here goes for a brevet or a cof-
> fin!" Whether this line occurred to him spontaneously or whether
> he had rehearsed it is not known, but it does recall similar epi-
> grams. Colonel Bennet Riley, for instance, told Jefferson Davis that
> he would win a yellow sash or six feet of Mexican soil. Brigadier
> William J. Worth called to Zachary Taylor at Monterrey that he
> would have a grade or a grave. Navy Lt. William Barker Cush-
> ing was heard to say when he went off to sink the Confederate
> *Albemarle:* "Another stripe or a coffin." No doubt such sentiments
> have echoed across battlefields from Philippi to Guadalcanal and
> beyond. . . .
>
> Anyway, it is said that during the gestation of *Remembrance of
> Things Past* the author gradually became convinced of a frighten-
> ing psychological truth: Contrary to popular belief, people do not
> learn by experience. Instead, they respond to a particular stimu-

lus in a predictable way, and this repeatedly. Again, again, again, and again this undeviating, compulsive response may be observed. A brevet or a coffin. A yellow sash or six feet of Mexican soil. A grade or a grave. Again, again, again, and again, generation after generation, the dismal message reappears like writing on the wall.

They were, to be sure, in a high-risk profession, but perhaps we asked more than we ought of them, and perhaps they gave too little care to themselves.

My figures on these deaths are probably a little high. I omitted deaths that clearly did not seem related to military life, but I assumed that most early deaths were military-related. A young man from Vermont probably doesn't drown in the Rio Grande at age 25, in 1845, unless he gets to the Rio Grande. The figure I cited, then, includes early deaths in the period 1842–61, early deaths on both sides during the Civil War, and deaths at an early age in the three years (and in a few instances, to 1870) just after the war, when the deaths were, as best as I could guess, military-related. Of the 856 West Point graduates from 1842 through 1861, that is to say, 33 percent were dead by about 1868. Uncommon losses.

Of 56 in the graduating class of 1842, 20 died young. Among the survivors are some readily recognizable names: William Rosecrans, Abner Doubleday, Daniel Hill, James Longstreet. Were there better men among the dead? Among 39 graduates in the class of 1843 (Lieutenant Chadbourne's class), 16 died young. U. S. Grant was a notable survivor. Was there a better among the dead? Twelve of the 25 graduates in the class of 1844 died young. Of 41 graduates in the class of 1845, 21 died .young. By percentage, this class was the hardest hit. From 59 graduates in the class of 1846, 26 died young. This class lost the greatest number, among them Stonewall Jackson. Among the survivors were George McClellan and George Pickett, who led the famous charge at Gettysburg. Of 38 graduates in the class of 1847, 11 died young. Eighteen of the 38 graduates in the class of 1848 died young. Among 43 graduates in the class of 1849, 11 died young.

Twelve of the 44 graduates in the class of 1850 died young, and 13 of the 42 graduates in the class of 1851. Eight of the 43 graduates of 1852 died young. Of 52 graduates in the class of 1853, 16 died young. Among the survivors were Philip Sheridan and John Bell Hood. Twenty of the 46 graduates in the class of 1854 died young, among them James Ewell Brown Stuart. Seven of the 34 graduates in the class of 1855 died young. James McNeill Whistler was admitted to the academy with this class in 1851 but did not finish. Of 49 graduates in the class of 1856, 17 died young. Among the survivors was James William Forsyth, who would be commanding officer at Wounded Knee in its time of infamy. Ten graduates of the 38 in the class of 1857 died young. Among the survivors were Henry Martyn Robert, who later wrote *Robert's Rules of Order*, and Marcus Albert Reno, who also survived Custer's engagement at the Little Big Horn. Eleven of 27 graduates in the class of 1858 died young, and 6 of 22 in the class of 1859.

Of 41 graduates in the class of 1860, 12 died young. Two classes were graduated in 1861. In the May 1861 class there were 45 graduates. Eight died young. In the June 1861 class there were 34 graduates. Nine died young. Among the survivors, though not for long, was George Armstrong Custer, last in his class.

I have been extravagant in my counting. I've made no attempt, as some have done for later wars, to distinguish between "battle deaths" and "other deaths," except where I thought it was obviously necessary to do so. The figures I have cited, then, are high, but even if I err by a hundred or two, the remainder is too much.

(Sad anomalies and losses occur in other ways: I think of the young men who died in duels, two from the class of 1850; of those who served the Confederacy and survived, needing an army, and found their way to Egypt, to Peru, to Nicaragua; of the young man who resigned and found a war in Cuba, only to die there shortly, in 1851.)

I expect it would not be hard to find another group that lost as much, or more. Someone always dies sooner and harder. That's the way it is with others; they die sometimes while we sometimes live. Still, I wanted to take notice, even if I have not rehearsed their names. Mostly, we kill other people because we do not know that they are people, and they are not people because we do not notice. Perhaps if we took a little notice a little sooner, we'd some day come to study war no more.

Seven

Looking Again and Seeing Susan Miles of San Angelo

Susan Miles of San Angelo did all the work. She was looking for Lieutenant Chadbourne before I knew who he was. She almost found him. She raised him, if not from the dead, at least from the anonymous.

I don't know her. I know her. I will never know her. If I had world enough and time, I'd like to follow her, to learn more about her than I have learned. What did she tell in files that I have not seen? I probably won't get around to looking, but she left interesting tracks.

Eight

What She Perhaps Saw

I don't know what she saw. I can't see through her eyes. I know her, but I don't know her and never will.

But I can follow the tracks she left.

Before long, I began to think that I needed to go to San Angelo again, to turn southwest out of Abilene and, after a while, to drive by the low, vague bluff where the marker for Fort Chadbourne is, to ease on down through Bronte and Tennyson to San Angelo and Fort Concho, where maybe I could ask someone why the trace of Lieutenant Chadbourne was there, at the wrong fort. But I didn't expect Miss Miles.

I didn't take it as a task to go to San Angelo. Mindy, my younger daughter, still lived there with Bin, her husband, and Andrew, their son, who was just past his first birthday. No bother at all, you see, to go to San Angelo.

And I was, by this time, curious to know how his sword and sword belt and, I thought, his tunic came to be in the little museum housed in post headquarters. On Tuesday, August 4, 1987, I called Fort Concho. I'm sorry that I don't know who answered. Maybe she was a receptionist or other staff member. When I sort of explained—which was all I could do—what I thought I was trying to learn, she reckoned that I needed to talk to Wayne Daniel, the librarian and archivist at Fort Concho. When it turned out that he was out on the grounds of the post, digging out what was left of a foundation, she reckoned that I needed to talk to Kathleen Roland, the curator of collections. She was in and I talked to her, but she disclaimed any special knowledge of the Chadbourne artifacts and told me that it was all owed to Susan Miles and that I should talk to Katharine Waring, of the Tom Green County Historical Society, who could tell me about Susan Miles.

I hadn't expected Miss Miles, but I called Katharine Waring and made an appointment to see her on Saturday, August 8, 1987. No problem, you see, to go to San Angelo.

Nine

The Tracks They Left

Miss Waring met me at Fort Concho. She was on the porch of the old officer's quarters that now serves as office, library, and repository for the Tom Green County Historical Association. She had come early and had already opened the doors and windows to let in the little breeze. Later, while I read, she swept and cleaned the office.

I tried to explain myself, though I wasn't sure I could then, and am not much surer now. What it came to then was simple enough to say, if not to explain: I needed to know about Lieutenant Chadbourne. I told her that I had written a short piece about him (chapter 2) without knowing much, but now I needed to know more.

We visited awhile. She told me about the County Historical Society. I told her about my daughter and son-in-law and grandson. I told her that they enjoyed San Angelo.

After a while, I asked her about the sword and the sword belt and, I thought, the tunic. I asked her how they came to be at Fort Concho and told her what Kathleen Roland had said, that Miss Waring would be the one to tell me.

She shrugged away any self-importance and said that it was all because of Susan Miles. "She wanted to know," she said. "Don't you see?"

I wish I could testify that those were her very words, but I can't. I think they catch her sense, but I won't try to say her words again.

Miss Waring went on to tell me a little about why Miss Miles wanted to know. She reminded me that men from Fort Chadbourne had come to help establish Fort Concho. She reminded me that one of the principal streets through downtown San Angelo is Chadbourne Street. I'd guess Miss Miles knew that Fort Chadbourne was already important to Fort Concho and San Angelo, though most didn't know it; or if they knew it, they didn't know why. I'd guess she thought that if Fort Chadbourne was important, then Lieutenant Chadbourne was important. Perhaps she thought, in the late 1940s and early 1950s when folks were just getting started in their efforts to save and to restore Fort Concho, that somebody ought to find out more, too, about Fort Chadbourne and Lieutenant Chadbourne, else some story wouldn't be complete.

Then Miss Waring told me that the County Historical Society still had some of Miss Miles's papers. She said I could see them if I wished.

I didn't know Miss Miles then and don't know her now, but I thought I had begun to sense her, to catch a trace of her. Most of us, I expect, have known someone a little like her—a schoolteacher, perhaps, or a Sunday school teacher, or someone mistakenly dismissed as a mere "club woman." Such women—at least, I'm convinced, those in the American South and West—may not have cleared and plowed the fields, but they did create and keep the culture, sometimes as teachers but always as *movers*, people who made and kept history without being acknowledged by history. In churches, for example, preachers and elders and deacons do important stuff, but it's always some group of women that does the church's real daily work.

In schools, principals have done the public posing, but women

have done the work. In one way or another, I expect, women have turned gatherings of folks, some drunk and disorderly, into towns and cities. On any college campus in the country, some (usually) small groups of women—secretaries, registrars, administrative assistants, advising counselors—know, maintain, and promote the college's work. Each is superbly well suited to be a major administrator; all are forever denied advancement because they lack what some are pleased to call "the terminal degree" or "the appropriate credentials." I didn't know Miss Miles then and don't know her now, but I thought I had begun to see her traces. I was to learn shortly that when she wanted to know something, she was likely to be persistent.

At least some of her files remained. Miss Waring said that I could see them.

She had already cleared a place for me at a table in the middle of the building, where, she said, a bit of draft would come through. She brought two boxes and set them on the table before me.

I didn't know that I was about to see the momentous. I had come prepared to take notes, and I still have the notes, but because I didn't know then that everything mattered, I didn't take note of everything carefully. The two boxes, for example. I believe that the box on top was about the size of the box that a ream of good paper comes in. The second box, I believe, was the same size around but not as deep. I opened the top box.

Inside, on top, was a book, an 1822 Paris edition of Virgil's *Bucolics*, *Georgics*, and *Aeneid*. On the inside of its front cover, written by hand, was "23rd of August." On the second flyleaf, this signature appeared:

T. L. Chadbourne
Eastport
1837

His signature appeared again on the title page.

She was looking for Lieutenant Chadbourne before I knew who he was. She almost found him. She raised him, if not from the dead, at least from the anonymous.

With the next item, the first below the book, my notes fail me almost completely. All my notes say is "S Ex Doc, 1849–1850, vol. 14, pp. 13–25." I cannot right now remember whether the box contains only Miss Miles's notation of the document or a reproduction of the noted pages from the document. I assume that the note refers to Senate Executive Document 64 (31st Congress, 1st Session, 1849–50), an extensive report from the secretary of war that includes some now well-known accounts: the reconnaissance by Brevet Lieutenant Colonel J. E. Johnson and others (including Samuel G. French, Lieutenant Chadbourne's classmate) of routes from San Angelo to El Paso, Captain Marcy's trip from Fort Smith to Santa Fe, Lieutenant J. H. Simpson's expedition into Navajo country, and Lieutenant W. H. C. Whiting's reconnaissance up across Texas. The pages designated in Miss Miles's file box, if I have correctly identified the document, are from that part of Lieutenant Colonel Johnson's report that tells about the country around where Fort Chadbourne and Fort Concho would come to be.

The book surprised me, but the next item was more surprising. It was a letter, and as I read it I learned that Miss Miles had exchanged letters with surviving members of the Chadbourne family in 1951. This letter, dated October 27, 1951, is to Miss Miles from Mrs. Frederick W. Denton, return address the Hotel Puritan, 390 Commonwealth Avenue, Boston, Massachusetts. She writes: "I am sure that such of us of the Chadbourne family as are left will feel grateful for your effort to preserve the name and reputation of one of them who apparently earned the honor now being granted him." She remembers, she says, seeing a letter from Lieutenant-to-be Chadbourne, written home shortly before he was graduated from the United States Military Academy. The letter, she says, expresses his regret that, because of the need to move from the academy to his first post, he will have to sell his horse and his piano. She identifies herself: Theodore Lincoln Chadbourne, dead in 1846, was her uncle, though she still lives in 1951. Her father, it turns out, was the seventh son of the family, about twenty years younger than his oldest brother, Theodore Lincoln. Mrs. Denton remembers, she believes, a trunk that belonged to the lieutenant, and for the first time I learn what family called him—she refers to it as "Uncle Lincoln's trunk."

Below Mrs. Denton's letter was another, from Theodore Lincoln Chadbourne, who identifies himself as the "nephew and namesake of my father's eldest brother, Lt. Theodore Lincoln Chadbourne, U.S.A." He believes that another descendant, T. L. Eschweiler of Milwaukee, has the lieutenant's sword.

My notes from the summer of 1987 now become more hurried. Today is Sunday, June 18, 1989. I can remember now—accurately, I believe—that by this point my notes were also becoming unreliable because I was beginning to believe that, for me, something notable was about to happen.

The next sheets—and by now I was into the smaller second box—showed that Miss Miles was looking intently for the lieutenant.

She wrote in July 1952 to the *Eastport Sentinel*, his hometown newspaper in Maine, to learn about him, only to find that the *Sentinel* files from 1832 to 1853 had been destroyed. She checked accounts of the Battle of Resaca de la Palma in the *Dictionary of American History* and in Justin Smith's *War with Mexico*. She learned long before I did that the *New York Herald* reported his death on May 26, 1846 (page 1, column 5). She checked Heitman's *Historical Register and Dictionary of the United States Army*, and from at least 1950 she was hunting newspaper reports and book citations, and she was appealing to state archives from Texas to Maine, and to the archivists at the Military Academy and in Washington. I guess she wanted to know.

Up to here I had only notes, and they were getting hurried. I looked deeper into the box, back in August 1987, and saw that there were many pages to go. A quick count showed 83 pages of letters to Miss Miles and many photostats. I was afraid I'd miss something, as I am now. I asked Miss Waring if I could come back and photocopy the rest. She said I could. I arranged to meet her on Monday, August 17—no problem, you remember, to go to San Angelo. I was afraid I'd miss something, and I had seen what was beneath the letters to her and the photostats.

At the bottom of the second box were Lieutenant Chadbourne's letters. Not photostats. His letters. On his paper, in his hand.

Ten

Backtracking along the
Trail She Made

In the week I had before I was to photocopy the remaining papers, I started trying to be both serious and systematic in searching for sources that might tell me about Lieutenant Chadbourne. By now, I might have known: in the *West Texas Historical Association Year Book* (volume 41, October 1965), she had published a paper, "Lieutenant Theodore Lincoln Chadbourne." It rests on her own study and on the lieutenant's letters, and I depend upon it.

On Monday, August 17, 1987, I went back and copied the files, including his letters. Colonel (ret.) Robert Byrns, president of the Tom Green County Historical Society, gave me a letter granting me permission to use the material.

Before I left, I made another quick tour of the fort. In the gift shop over in one of the enlisted men's barracks I chanced upon Robert W. Frazier's *Forts of the West*, which I had known about but entirely forgotten. I don't believe much in signs and portents, but I do remember thinking that it looked like I ought to get busy hunting Lieutenant Chadbourne. Indications were all around me.

Since I was there and might not be again for a while, I stopped by the Fort Concho headquarters building and the museum there to look one more time at his gear. His sword was there, and his sword belt, but this time I realized that his tunic

wasn't there. Under the sword belt there was only blue cloth.
I looked some more and after a while came away, and now, in
June 1989, I'm trying to look again.

In her paper Miss Miles takes no credit:

> In 1952 through contact with Dr. T. L. Chadbourne, aging nephew
> and namesake of Lieutenant Chadbourne, and shortly after with
> his widow, the Tom Green County Historical Society fell heir to the
> small collection of letters from and to the great soldier, covering a
> period of seven years, 1839–1846. A great nephew sent background
> data, another the Lieutenant's sword, and present occupants of the
> Chadbourne home in Eastport, Maine, sent pictures of the house
> and grounds.

She, of course, had more than a little to do with all of that,
though she is removed from her own account.

She began tentatively. She did not live next door to a major,
or even a large, library. In most instances, her files show only
replies to her letters. Either she did not make copies of her own
inquiries, or they've been lost, or she thought they didn't matter. At any rate, to start with, she apparently wrote to the War
Department, and on April 20, 1948, received this reply:

Miss Susan Miles
112 No/Irving Street
San Angelo, Texas

The records show that Heitman's Historical Register and Dictionary of the United States Army (1789–1903) contains a record
of Lieutenant Theodore Lincoln Chadbourne of Maine, who was
killed 9 May 1846 at the Battle of Resaca de la Palma, Texas, in the
Mexican War. This publication can be [found in] most large public
libraries.

/s/ Edward F. Witsell
EDWARD F. WITSELL
Major General
The Adjutant General

A handwritten note in the margin—I assume hers—indicates
that on April 26, 1948, she wrote to the University of Texas.

On April 30, 1948, she got a reply. Kathleen Blow, of the Reference Department at the University of Texas Library, wrote
to her, giving references to Gardner's *Dictionary of All Persons Who Have Been Commissioned, or Have Been Appointed*

and Served, in the Army of the United States (1853), to Powell's
*List of Officers of the Army of the United States from 1799 to
1900,* and to Heitman's *Historical Register and Dictionary of
the United States Army, 1903.*

On June 30, 1948, she received a letter from the Eastport
Public Library Association, Eastport, Maine:

> Dear Mrs. Miles:
>
> I was surprised to receive your postal saying that you had received
> no information on Lieutenant Theodore Chadbourne. There was
> nothing pertaining to him in the library so I passed your letter to the
> President of the board of directors as I knew the family had been
> friends of the Chadbournes. He promised to attend to it, and I am
> sorry that he neglected it. I remembered there was a monument at
> the cemetery, so I have copied the inscription on it for you. If you
> should need further information there is a Mrs. Arthur Lincoln of
> Dennysville Me who is a relative I think.
>
> Please forgive the delay it was not intentional.
>
> > Cordially,
> >
> > Mrs. Martha J. Thompson, Librarian
> > 15 Water St.

By Mrs. Thompson's name there is a handwritten note—I assume it's Miss Miles again—that says, "ack 7/8/48." In the
margin by Mrs. Lincoln's name are three notes: "wrote 7/8/48,
6/20/50, 8/28/51." Attached to the letter is the following copy
of the inscriptions on the marble shaft:

> Theodore Lincoln Chadbourne
> Lieut. 8th Infantry U.S.A.
> Born at Eastport
> August 2, 1822
> Graduated at Military Academy
> West Point, 1843
> Fell in the battle of
> Resaca de la Palma
> May 9, 1846
> *On West side of marble shaft*
>
> His last acts are part of his country's
> History
> The Memory

of his frank and ingenuous disposition
of his love of excellence and devotion to duty
and of his high and generous aims
is deeply surgraved on the hearts
of the friends and associates
of his youth by whom this monument
has been raised.
On the east side of the marble shaft.

On another side of the shaft is the following information:

Theodore Lincoln Chadbourne was the eldest son of Ichabod Rollins Chadbourne, who was the 16th Representative of Eastport, chosen in 1839 and re-elected the following year, a Whig in his politics; he (Ichabod) was the son of Jonathan Chesley and Elizabeth (Rollins) Chadbourne, born at South Berwick, Maine, Jan. 8th, 1707, and he was descended from Humphrey Chadbourne, who was one of the leaders of the first settlers on the Piscataqua; and his grandfather, Benjamin Chadbourne, was prominent in the Revolutionary period, having represented South Berwick for 16 years in the General Court of Massachusetts.

Mr. Ichabod R. Chadbourne graduated at Dartmouth College in 1808, studied law with George Wallingford at Kennebunk and Daniel Davis at Boston, was admitted to the Suffolk bar in 1812 and came to Eastport soon after. His wife was Hannah Lincoln— Ichabod died at Eastport Dec. 8th, 1855.

Ichabod's eldest son, Theodore Lincoln Chadbourne, was graduated at West Point in the same class with General Grant, was appointed 2nd Lieut. in the 8th U.S. Infantry, and fell at the battle of Resaca de la Palma, in Mexico, May 9th, 1846—his remains were brought to Eastport for burial; and the friends and associates of his youth erected a monument to his memory in the cemetery, which bears an inscription written by Dr. Isaac Ray, a former resident and friend of the family.

After this, there is silence for two years, though I think it's file silence, not real silence, for then she received a letter from the United States Military Academy:

UNITED STATES MILITARY ACADEMY
WEST POINT, NEW YORK

26 June, 1950

Miss Susan Miles
112 North Irving Street
San Angelo, Texas

Dear Miss Miles:

Reference your letter of 20 June 1950, the records of this Headquarters indicate that Lieutenant Theodore L. Chadbourne was admitted to the United States Military Academy as a cadet from the United States at Large on 1 September 1839 at the age of 17 years and 3 months. He was graduated No. 15 in a class of 39 members and commissioned as Bvt. 2d Lieutenant, 2d Infantry, in the United States Army on 1 July 1843.

Lieutenant Chadbourne served in garrison at Fort Niagara, New York from 1843 until 1845. He was promoted to 2d Lieutenant, 8th Infantry, on 10 September 1845. Lieutenant Chadbourne served in the Military Occupation of Texas, 1845–46; and in the War with Mexico, 1846, being engaged in the Battle of Palo Alto, 8 May 1846, and the Battle of Resaca-de-la-Palma, where, after distinguishing himself at the head of his command, he was killed on 9 May 1846, at the age of 23 years.

I regret that we do not have a picture of Lieutenant Chadbourne

on file at this Headquarters. The above is the only available information of record.

Sincerely yours,

R. S. NOURSE
Colonel, AGD
Adjutant General

She corrected the letter. Where it says that he entered the
academy at the age of 17 years and 3 months, she has written
in the margin "1 month—was born Aug. 2."

Then she received an answer to the letters she had written
to Mrs. Arthur Lincoln on 7/8/48 or 6/20/50 or 8/28/51. A letter from Calais Regional Hospital, Calais, Maine, dated September 5, 1951, came from Mrs. Ida L. Brown, who identifies
herself as Mrs. Lincoln's sister-in-law:

> Dear Mrs. Miles,
>
> Mrs. Lincoln passed away last March—I do not remember see-
> ing any photographs of Lt. Chadbourne or anything connected with
> him among her papers—She was 94 yrs. of age and had retired to
> a convalescent home to end her days—she had only been there a
> few weeks when she fell and broke her hip—You might write to
> Dr. Thomas L. Chadbourne who lives in Vinton-Ohio—it is either
> Ohio or Iowa—but I think Ohio—you can check up on it—Sorry
> not be able to give you any further information but I am in the
> hospital myself for a checkup and treatment.

Marginal notes indicate that Miss Miles wrote to Dr. Chadbourne on September 10, 1951.

On September 11, 1951, she received an answer from the
Library of Congress:

THE LIBRARY OF CONGRESS
Washington 25, D.C.

Reference Department
Serials Division

September 11, 1951

Dear Miss Miles:

Your letter of August 28, 1951, requesting information concerning Lt. Theodore Lincoln Chadbourne, has been referred to the
Series Division for attention and reply.

I regret to report that we have been unable to locate any news-

paper accounts concerning Lt. Chadbourne other than the following item which was published in *The Daily Picayune*, New Orleans,
May 19, 1846, page 4, column 1:

". . . The officers killed on the field were Lieut. Inges of 2nd
dragoons, Lieut. Coheran of the 4th infantry, and Lieut. Chadbourne of the 8th infantry. . . ."

The above article also appeared in *The New York Herald*, May 26,
1846, page 1, column 5, and *The Mobile Register and Journal*,
May 19, 1846, page 2, column 3.

The Library's newspaper collection does not include any files
from Texas for this period. According to the *Union List of Newspapers* the Texas State Library, Austin, has the *Texas Democrat*,
Austin, and the University of Texas, Austin, has the *Standard*,
Clarksville, for 1846.

Very truly yours,

Clyde S. Edwards
Chief, Serials Division

Miss Susan Miles
112 North Irving Street
San Angelo, Texas

At the same time she wrote to the Library of Congress, she
apparently also wrote to the National Archives and Records
Service of the General Services Administration:

GENERAL SERVICES ADMINISTRATION
National Archives and Records Service
Washington 25, D.C.

September 25, 1951

Miss Susan Miles
112 North Irving Street
San Angelo, Texas

Dear Miss Miles:

This is in reply to your request of August 28, 1951, for information
concerning Lieutenant Theodore Chadbourne.

A search has been made of pertinent records in the National Archives and no picture has been found of Lieutenant Chadbourne.
No picture of him is listed in the "Portrait Index" of the American Library Association, which is the best source for portraits in
published works prior to 1900. It is suggested that you address a
request to Miss Marion Rouse, Maine Historical Society, Congress

Square, Portland, Maine. There may be a picture of Lieutenant
Chadbourne among the society's collection of pictures of local per-
sonages.

A careful search of the pension and bounty-land records of the
Veterans' Administration in the National Archives fails to reveal a
file for the soldier in whom you are interested.

The records of the War Department in the National Archives
cited below may be of interest to you. Negative photostatic copies
of these documents can be furnished at the following costs:

Letter dated July 21, 1843, from Chadbourne to The Adju-
tant General, reporting birthplace and enclosing Oath .60
Letter dated February 28, 1845, from Chadbourne to The
Adjutant General, acknowledging commission .30

Letter dated August 19, 1845, from Chadbourne to The
Adjutant General, protesting the loss of a promotion by
the filling of a vacancy by a civilian .90

Letter dated September 9, 1845, from Chadbourne to The
Adjutant General, on above subject 1.20

Letter dated August 26, 1845, Chadbourne's father to
President James K. Polk, on above subject .90

Letter dated September 14, 1845, Chadbourne to The
Adjutant General, acknowledging promotion and orders .90

Letter dated March 29, 1846, Chadbourne to The Adjutant
General, acknowledging commission .30

Letter dated May 9, 1846, Brig. Gen. Zachary Taylor to The
Adjutant General, describing the battle of Matamoros, in
which he mentions the death of Chadbourne .90

If you wish to order the photostats, please send your remittance in
the proper amount to the National Archives in the form of a check
or money order *made payable to the Treasurer of the United States.*

Sincerely yours,

Nelson M. Blake
For Dallas Irvine
Chief Archivist
War Records Branch

Her marginal note indicates that she wrote to the Maine Historical Society on October 3, 1951, and ordered the archival
material on November 11, 1951. A following note from the

General Services Administration says only, "We take pleasure in sending you the photographic reproductions that you recently requested." The first attachment, a photostatic letter, reads as follows:

Eastport Me July 21 1843

Sir—

Agreeably to par 6th General Orders No 42 I have the honor to report as my birthplace the town of Eastport, St. of Maine —I was appointed from the same State—

Your Obed't Serv't
Theodore L. Chadbourne
brevet 2d Lieut 2d Infantry

Gen R. Jones
Adjutant General U.S. Army

Attached to this, with the same date, is his oath:

I, Theodore L. Chadbourne, appointed a Brevet 2nd Lieutenant in the Army of the United States, do solemnly swear, or affirm, that I will bear true allegiance to the United States of America, and that I will serve them honestly and faithfully against all their enemies or opposers whatsoever; and observe and obey the orders of the President of the United States, and the orders of the Officers appointed over me, according to the Rules and Articles for the government of the Armies of the United States.

Sworn to and subscribed before   /s/ Theodore L. Chadbourne
me at Eastport,   bvt 2d Lieut 2d Inf'y
this 21 day of July, 1843

But I can't make out the name of the justice of the peace. Then, from Fort Niagara, his first duty station, on February 28, 1845, he wrote accepting his commission. I have not yet learned why there was such a long delay.

The next item in the archival materials reveals that the young brevet second lieutenant was indignant. On August 19, 1845, he wrote to the adjutant general in protest: a position that he thinks properly his—it entailed a promotion to second lieutenant in the 7th Infantry—has been given to a civilian named Quimby. On August 25, 1845, his father joined him in protest, writing directly to President Polk:

. . . I have a son Theodore Lincoln Chadbourne who is a Brevet 2d Lt. 2d Infantry, Ft. Niagara, who is the first on the list of Brevets and who according to the rules and regulations of the army and invariable usage was entitled to the place you have filled by the appointment of a person out of the line of the army.

I confess I was incredulous when I read the account as I was unwilling to believe that the President had committed an act which would be considered a very strong exercise of power if not of great injustice and as the President has been a military man he must know how tenacious officers are of their rank and how important to the army it is that such a feeling should be respected . . .

Then, since he had received no reply to his earlier letter, Lieutenant Chadbourne wrote again to the adjutant general on September 9, 1845. The letter is not gentle:

Sir:

I have the honor to inform you that I addressed a letter to Headquarters during the latter part of last month, the contents of which related to the appointment by the President of a citizen to fill the vacancy in the Infantry which by regulation belongs to me. After waiting what I suppose a reasonable length of time for an answer, from which I might learn whether or not I can obtain from Headquarters the information sought for concerning the appointment; and it being a matter in which I am very deeply interested, I make this second communication in the hope of learning whether any notice is to be taken of my first one. If I am to expect no answer, I respectfully request that you would inform me of it, as it may make an important difference in the course I shall pursue in relation to the matter in question. I shall more easily overcome the reluctance which I feel in troubling the General in chief by asking for information which I think very probable he may be entirely unable to give; for the reason that the grievance complained of is one affecting in the most serious manner one of the dearest rights of every member of the Army. It would be wasting words to attempt to enlarge upon the consequences of an act which you must of course be so much better able to trace out and appreciate than myself.

I thought (but my inexperience may have led me astray) that my first step should be to lay my complaint officially before the Commander in chief; being at least certain of his disposition to sympathize with even the lowest member of his army, who has suffered an undeserved injury; and his readiness to protect by all means in his power the rights of all under his command. The President has undoubtedly the *power* to deprive me at any moment of the commission which I now hold, without assigning or being able to assign any reason whatever for the act; so he has the power to pursue the course he did in depriving me of the commission which by regulation belonged to me; and were he this day to strike my name from the rolls of the Army, without cause, the second wrong would not be thought by me a greater one than the first, and less easy to be borne without complaint or remonstrance. I believe it my duty, one which I owe to my comrades of my own rank, as well as to myself, to complain of and to resist this act by every means in my power; and if I unfortunately learn that my hopes of promotion are liable to be blasted by a repetition of such acts, I must affirm, and I cannot see how anyone in the army can differ with me, that any commission of whatever rank, upon such conditions, is not to be desired.

Very respectfully
I am sir
Your obd't servant

T. L. Chadbourne
Bv't 2nd Lt. 2nd Infy.

As Miss Miles puts it in her paper, he threw his glove in Washington's face. Eventually, it turned out well for him: he got his promotion and a reply on October 13, 1845, from Adjutant General Jones, who concluded, "No one in the Army or out of it, I may add, can read your letter without commending the temper in which you write as well as the sentiments and justness of the views expressed." Or, eventually, perhaps it didn't turn out well; the promotion to second lieutenant and to the 8th Infantry took him to Resaca de la Palma.

Before the reply from Adjutant General Jones had come, Lieutenant Chadbourne had received his promotion and had written again to the adjutant general:

Sir:

I have the honor to inform you that I have this day received a communication from the Secretary of War, notifying me of my promotion by the President of the United States to the 8th Regiment of Infantry as a second Lieutenant, and advising me to join my XXXXXXX without delay, at the Bay of Aransas, Texas.

I have the honor
to be very respectfully
Your Obd't Serv't,
/s/ T. L. Chadbourne
2d Lt. Infantry

Where the Xs occur above, I believe that he first wrote *company*
and then wrote *regiment* over that.

On March 29, 1846, from the Camp Opposite Matamoros, he wrote to the adjutant general, acknowledging receipt of his commission.

The last item among the photostats from Washington in Miss Miles's collection is part of General Taylor's report for May 9, 1846; in it he describes the day's battle and mentions the death of Lieutenant Chadbourne.

Then her file returns to Miss Miles's present. She heard again, on October 3, 1951, the same day she wrote to the Maine Historical Society, from Martha Thompson, librarian at Eastport:

EASTPORT PUBLIC LIBRARY ASSOCIATION
Eastport, Maine
Miss Susan Miles Exec Secy

Dear Miss Miles:

After some delay your letter has reached me from the Library Association. I have been able to find two more names, but do not have strict numbers. They are as follows.

Mrs. Hannah Chadbourne Denton, Houghton, Michigan
and Mrs. Bruce Harkness, Houghton, Michigan.

The monument was covered with moss, but I have the promise of a snapshot, as soon as it can be cleared.

I hope that this information will be of some service. There was a Miss Rose Chadbourne who lived formerly in Eastport but so far have not been successful in finding an address. Will mail the "snaps" as soon as I receive them.

Cordially,

Mrs. Martha Thompson, Librarian

Miss Miles's marginal notes indicate that she acknowledged the letter on October 13, 1951, and that she wrote on October 8, 1951, to both of the women named in the letter. Then, very shortly, this letter, dated October 9, 1951, arrived (the photograph mentioned is now in the display case at Fort Concho), addressed to Susan Wills:

EASTPORT PUBLIC LIBRARY ASSOCIATION
EASTPORT - MAINE

Miss Susan Wills
Executive Secretary,
Tom Green County Hist. Soc.,
112 North Irving St.,
San Angelo, Texas

Dear Miss Wills:

Your recent letter to the Eastport Public Library Association, with newspaper clipping showing the building to be dedicated in memory of Thomas Lincoln Chadbourne, fell into my hands.

Your request for a picture of the monument took me to the cemetery. The monument was so moss covered that no picture would have shown the inscriptions. Our City Manager, Mr. W. S. Alexander, whose grandfather fought in the Civil War, who was in World War One himself, and whose only son was killed at Okinawa, was most interested in your letter and in securing a picture of the monument. He sent the City crew and free of charge they cleaned the monument. Then our local photographer, a World War I veteran, for a nominal fee took the print which I am sending you under separate cover. We think it a fine picture of the monument. With the inscription on two sides, the picture was taken at an angle to show both sides and with a glass I think you can decipher the inscriptions, which Mrs. Thompson, our Librarian, has already sent you.

It is not yet quite clear to me why San Angelo was and is interested in Lt. Chadbourne. Is the city near Resaca de la Palma?

A Thomas Chadbourne, a nephew, I think, of Lt. Chadbourne made a great deal of money in the celebrated Calumet and Hecla Copper mine in Houghton, Mich. Your bringing this incident to our attention has roused interest and our City Manager is going to try and contact relatives of Thomas Chadbourne and secure perpetual care for the cemetery lot. You will note that the grass around the lot has not been cared for.

I wrote a little account of all this for our local paper which comes out this week and I will send you a copy. I did not ask for any further information about the Chadbournes as I think everyone in town who has any such knowledge has been contacted. Mrs. Thompson has the past week sent you, I think, two names of Thos. Chadbourne relatives in Houghton.

I shall be interested in hearing from you.

Very truly yours,

(Mrs. Wm. C. Beale)
Sec'y Eastport Public

Almost immediately afterward, Miss Miles received a letter dated October 10, 1951, from a new actor in the story. Is
it too much, do you think, to imagine that, maybe, her throat
tightened a little when she read the reference to "certain such
objects which the present owners might consider leaving to a
proper museum"?

T. L. Chadbourne, M.D.
Vinton, Iowa

October 10, 1951

Miss Susan Miles
Tom Green Historical Society
San Angelo, Texas

Dear Miss Miles:

The circumstances are such that I cannot help being much interested in your letter of the tenth September.

I am called Theodore Lincoln Chadbourne and am the nephew
and namesake of my father's eldest brother, Lt. Theodore Lincoln
Chadbourne, U.S.A. This means that I have had ample opportunity
to know about any memorials left by my uncle.

I am very sure there is no picture of him in existence.

I should be interested to know what sort of facilities for the preservation of physical objects your historical society has or may have
in the future. There are certain such objects which the present
owners might consider leaving to a proper museum. Information
on this point would interest me very much.

Do you have a copy of the inscription on the memorial obelisk in
the cemetery in Eastport? I could send you this very heart warming
tribute.

Sorry about the lack of picture, but shall be interested in your
reply.

Very sincerely yours,

T. L. Chadbourne

Others appear. In a letter dated October 27, 1951, Hannah C.
Denton wrote. She had been recommended to Miss Miles by
Martha Thompson, the librarian at Eastport:

Oct. 27

Mrs. Frederick W. Denton
Hotel Puritan
390 Commonwealth Avenue
Boston, Massachusetts

Dear Miss Miles—

Your letter was forwarded to me from Houghton where I lived for many years but now live at the above address.

My cousin Dr. Theodore Lincoln Chadbourne died recently but I have written his widow asking if her husband had any picture of Lieut. Chadbourne. I have also written my nephew H. Lincoln Chadbourne who lives in California if any such pictures were found among his father's papers. His father died a year ago—I know of no other Chadbournes of the family of Lieut. Chadbourne. I am sure that such of us of the Chadbourne family as are left will feel grateful for your effort to preserve the name and reputation of one of them who apparently earned the honor now being granted him.

In a letter to his father written just before his graduation from West Point Lt. Chadbourne expressed great regret at having to sell his horse and his piano before leaving. These things would now seem strange property for a West Pointer to have! I will write you the result of my two inquiring letters.

Sincerely yours,

Hannah C. Denton

A few days later, Mrs. Denton wrote again:

Nov. 9 [1951]

Dear Miss Miles:

It seems evident that there is nothing left in the possession of relatives of Lt. Chadbourne that ever, in any way, was a concern of his, or concerned with him. In digging into my memory I've found, and left behind me in a former home an old trunk which was known in the family as "Uncle Lincoln's sole-leather trunk"—I had seen it many times in our garret and when I was dismantling (I suppose that's the word) the house I examined the little trunk carefully to see why it was known as "sole leather"—about the size of a small modern steamer trunk it did look as if it had been made of one piece of leather, but was of course dilapidated. It was discarded with many other things that probably had been considered precious many years before. My father, the seventh son, was at least 20 years younger than his brother Lincoln. But no, I remember now that a cousin of mine, now dead, had Uncle Lincoln's sword, now perhaps owned by one of his sons—In the uniform of that time there was, I think, a white belt around the waist, and a white strap extending from the belt diagonally over the left [right] shoulder. On that strap was embroidered some sort of ornament, like a daisy, which was placed directly over the heart of the wearer and I think I remem-

ber clearly in the center of that flower-like ornament was the bullet
hole of the bullet that killed him.

I don't know why it has taken so long for me to recall this but I've
not seen it for years. The present owner is, I think, also Theodore
Lincoln, and the last name Eschweiler, the address Ashland, Wisconsin. I'm not sure he has the sword and I'm, of course, not in the
least certain that he would part with it. I think however that a letter
from you with the story, as you told it me, might accomplish more
than anything I could write. Stupid of me not to have thought of
this earlier.

Sincerely yours,

Hannah C. Denton

Miss Miles heard next, in a letter dated November 22, 1951,
from Dr. T. L. Chadbourne's widow:

Mrs. T. L. Chadbourne
Vinton
Iowa

Dear Miss Miles:

Thank you for your note of sympathy.

I'm sorry that all of the newspaper articles concerning Dr. Chad-
bourne have been given away and no more are available at the
Times office. This short notice [enclosed] was in the Cedar Rapids
Gazette.

As to Lt. Theodore Lincoln Chadbourne—we have nothing of
his—no photograph—except some personal letters.

This winter I'll look these up and send them to you.

Sincerely,

Virginia K. Chadbourne
Vinton,
Iowa

Nov. 22, 1951

I wonder how Miss Miles felt when she read that letter. I can
guess. I know how I felt when I found his letters in the box that
Miss Miles left. I judge that the original letters I saw are the
letters Mrs. Chadbourne refers to.

Very shortly, Mrs. Chadbourne wrote again:

Dear Miss Miles—

The address of Mr. Theodore L. Eschweiler is
Ashbourne

Hartland

Wisconsin

—Ashbourne is the name of their country estate.

Sincerely,

Virginia K. Chadbourne
Vinton, Iowa

Dec. 1, 1951

And then again the next day:

Dear Miss Miles—

In looking over the file of letters I find a number from Lt. Theodore Lincoln Chadbourne. There are also a number, more in fact from his father and brothers *to* him—These give very nice characterizations of him, and also tell where he is with his regiment and what they are doing. Do you want me to send you any of the letters pertaining to him? or only those written by him?

Sincerely,

Virginia K. Chadbourne

Dec. 2, 1951

Dare I imagine Miss Miles's reaction? Of course I do. *My* first impulse would have been to send a telegram saying "Hot Dawg! Send all of those babies." I would have resisted that impulse. Then I would have called and said something decorous; perhaps, "I surely hope that you'll be willing to send all of the letters."

Then Hannah Denton wrote again, on December 3, to be sure that Miss Miles had the correct address for Mr. Eschweiler in Wisconsin. Now Miss Miles heard from Theodore Lincoln Eschweiler himself, and for the first time it becomes plain what the city of San Angelo was about to do to honor Lieutenant Chadbourne. Can we assume that Miss Miles was prodding someone, ever so gently, perhaps, but ever so persistently? He enclosed a copy of a letter he had just written to Eastport:

December 11, 1951

Miss Susan Miles
112 North Irving Street
San Angelo, Texas

My Dear Miss Miles:

Thank you for your letter of November 13 which reached me a day or two ago after its trip to Vinton, Iowa.

Unfortunately I know of no photograph of Lieutenant Chadbourne at the present time but am contacting other members of the family who might possess such a photograph that could be copied and forwarded to you. We are all very much surprised and delighted to learn that San Angelo is perpetuating the memory of Lieutenant Chadbourne in such an outstanding manner.

The photograph of the sketch of the new Chadbourne Building now being erected in your city is most interesting and I sincerely hope I shall have an opportunity to see it when it is completed.

I am in possession of Lieutenant Chadbourne's sword which was given to me for safe keeping by the late Dr. T. L. Chadbourne of Vinton, Iowa. Dr. Chadbourne, however, requested that I will this sword to his son, Sandy. In view of this I am contacting Mrs. Chadbourne and Sandy to determine if they will be willing to have this sword put in your museum in San Angelo. When they have had time to think over this matter and express their wishes, you will hear from me again.

In the meantime I shall attempt to locate photographs and any other physical possessions of Lieutenant Chadbourne's which might be forwarded to your Historical Society.

Very sincerely yours,

TLE:lm   cc: Mrs. Denton
           Mr. Alexander
           Mrs. Chadbourne

ESCHWEILER and ESCHWEILER
Architects
720 East Mason Street
Milwaukee 2, Wisconsin

December 11, 1951

Mr. W. S. Alexander
Eastport, Maine

Dear Mr. Alexander:

Your letter of December 6 reached me yesterday. We are, of course, very much interested in cooperating with your city and creating a trust fund for the perpetual care of Lieutenant Chadbourne's monument.

Is the Hill Side Cemetery owned by the city of Eastport? Is there a trust fund now set up for the perpetual care of this cemetery? What is the city's estimate of the annual cost for the perpetual care of this lot and monument? Would it be possible for you to mail to me a copy of the photograph you mailed to the Historical Society of Texas?

Enclosed herewith is a copy of a letter just written to Miss Susan Miles which is self-explanatory.

We are anxious to cooperate with the citizens of San Angelo, Texas, as well as the city of Eastport and we would therefore appreciate the answers to the questions above before making decisions.

Yours very truly,

cc: Mrs. Denton
    Mrs. Chadbourne
    Miss Susan Miles

TLE/lm

The next item in Miss Miles's file is quiet, short, and uncommonly momentous:

Mrs. T. L. Chadbourne
Vinton
Iowa

Dear Miss Miles:

I sent you this morning—registered mail—the letters you want.

Sincerely,

Virginia K. Chadbourne

Dec. 12, 1951

Almost a month passes before the next item, another letter from Mrs. Chadbourne, appears:

Mrs. T. L. Chadbourne
Vinton
Iowa

Dear Miss Miles:

I have one more gift for the museum—if you want it. Dr. Chadbourne has been carrying a cane—a family cane, with inscription—Made from a tree splintered by cannon balls on the Resaca de la Palma field. I also have the letter (1851) which tells about it—made for Lt. TLC's father.

I am wondering who started these plans? Perhaps the County Historical Society?

Very sincerely,

Virginia K. Chadbourne

Jan. 8, 1951

The next letter in the file is also from Mrs. Chadbourne; it is dated January 17, 1952, and says briefly that she is sending the

cane and the letter, which is from General Sylvester Churchill,
who had known the family for a long time. The letter is not
legible in the photostatic form I have.

Shortly after that, Miss Miles heard again from Mr. Eschweiler, with good news about the sword:

ESCHWEILER and ESCHWEILER

Architects

720 East Mason Street

Milwaukee 2, Wisconsin

February 18, 1952

Miss Susan Miles
112 North Irving Street
San Angelo, Texas

Dear Miss Miles:

A second letter to you has been delayed for many reasons, but
the chief one being that a letter from Mrs. Chadbourne written a
month ago was lost in the mails until two or three days ago. In
this letter Mrs. Chadbourne stated that her son was kind enough to
relinquish his future right to the sword.

We are, therefore, advising that we are forwarding to you today,
under separate cover, Lt. Chadbourne's sword which has been in
my possession for the last twenty-five years, and I am happy to think
that it will be carefully cared for in San Angelo's museum.

Being of the wrong generation I have never learned of the heroic
deeds of my great uncle. Would your records list the heroic deeds
he performed in the Mexican War which prompted the city of San
Angelo to perpetuate his name? If it is not too much trouble, I would
appreciate having a record of this in my library.

Very sincerely yours,

TLE/lm

cc: Mrs. Denton
    Mrs. Chadbourne

Miss Miles's marginal note indicates that the sword arrived on
February 25, 1952.

Miss Miles wasn't through looking for Lieutenant Chadbourne, though. She still wanted a photograph.

MAINE HISTORICAL SOCIETY

485 Congress Street

(Incorporated February 5, 1822)

Portland 3, Maine, February 19, 1952

Miss Susan Miles
112 No. Irving Street
San Angelo, Texas

Dear Miss Miles:
    This is a very late answer to your letter of October 3. I am sorry. We have had a new addition built on to our library and have been moving books into it. During that process all other activities had to cease. Therefore my correspondence got far behind me.
    I have looked for a picture of Lt. Theodore Lincoln Chadbourne of Eastport, but have not found one.
    You might try the Maine State Library, State House, Augusta, Maine.

Sincerely yours,

Marian B. Rowe, Librarian

She followed that lead but learned nothing.

MAINE STATE LIBRARY
Augusta

March 3, 1952

Miss Susan Miles
Tom Green County Historical Society
112 No. Irving Street
San Angelo, Texas

Dear Miss Miles:
    We regret to report that we do not have a picture of Lieutenant Theodore L. Chadbourne of Eastport, Maine, who was killed in the Mexican war in 1846.
    Because of your many inquiries already made, we cannot offer a suggestion of where else you could go for help in your quest.

Very truly yours,

MAINE STATE LIBRARY
By Margaret A. Whelen

Research Librarian

mw

Then a new figure appears in Miss Miles's correspondence file, and he, too, has a gift. Since his letters are clipped together, I include them all here, though it means jumping ahead of some other letters that I will come to in a moment.

Alexander C. Brown
6074 Belmont Avenue

Miss Susan Miles
112 North Irving Str.
San Angelo, Texas

Dear Miss Miles:

I just ran across a volume of Virgil among some family books with the signature "T. L. Chadbourne, 1837." This would be my great uncle, Lt. Theodore Lincoln Chadbourne. As I understand that the city of San Angelo is interested in souveniers of him, I would be glad to contribute this one.

Very truly yours,

/s/ Alex C. Brown

His second letter includes a Chadbourne family tree:

May 15, 1952

Dear Miss Miles:

Thank you for your letter of May 12, from which I note that you would like to have the Virgil which belonged to Lt. T. L. Chadbourne. I am mailing it to you. The book was in the library of Dr. Theodore Lincoln Chadbourne, of Vinton, Ia., recently deceased.

To answer your questions about brothers and sisters and the like, I enclose some genealogical sheets from which you can obtain the information. . . .

Very sincerely yours,

/s/ Alex C. Brown

His third letter reveals that the Chadbourne Building in San Angelo has been opened and that the Chadbourne house in Eastport, Maine, is still standing in 1952:

November 8, 1952

Dear Miss Miles:

Thank you so much for the paper giving the account of the opening of the Chadbourne building. I can see that considerable research went into the preparation of the story, and I think you are to be complimented on it.

With regard to your postcard inviting comments on any errors, I did notice one. Lieutenant Chadbourne's mother was Hannah Lincoln of Dennysville, Maine, a village near Eastport. Her father, Theodore Lincoln, for whom the Lieutenant was named, was incorrectly referred to as General Theodore Lincoln in the story. It may however be of interest that he was the son of Major General Benjamin Lincoln, who you will be aware was one of Washington's generals in the Revolutionary War. The Lincoln house, which was the home of Theodore Lincoln, still stands in Dennysville, as does the Chadbourne house in Eastport.

Sincerely yours,

/s/ Alex Brown

Earlier than the third letter above, dated June 11, 1952, is a notable letter, the only letter in the file that was written *by* Miss Miles. I judge from it that the opening of the Chadbourne Building in San Angelo must have been timed to coincide with the centennial of the founding of Fort Chadbourne, which Miss Miles took to be November 5, 1852. Miss Miles's letter is hand-written, and the answer to it is typed at the bottom.

112 No. Irving Street
San Angelo, Texas

June 11, 1952

Editor Eastport Sentinel
Eastport, Maine

Dear Sir:
Do your files date back as far as May 9, 1846, when Lt. T. L. Chadbourne of Eastport was killed in the Mexican War? If so, could you send us copies of his death, funeral, etc.? We shall be glad to pay for photostatic copies.

Your library sent us a copy of your paper on October 11, 1951. Fort Chadbourne (in an adjoining county) was established in October, 1852, and by that time we wish to have as complete a file as we can obtain on Lt. Chadbourne. It is most regrettable that we cannot find a picture of him.

The Chadbourne Building here is nearing completion.

We very much appreciate the cooperation the citizens of Eastport have given us.

Sincerely,

(Miss) Susan Miles
Ex. Secy.
Tom Green County (Texas)
Historical Society

Alas, fires in Eastport have destroyed the continuity of bound volumes of The Sentinel. I suggest you write the Maine State Library,

State House, AUGUSTA-MAINE, for the information you seek. If you
can't be helped there, the Clerk of Courts, Machias Maine, may
have a complete file of Sentinels.

Sincerely yours,

Gerald Minto

Miss Miles followed the lead to the Maine State Library, but
to no avail:

MAINE STATE LIBRARY
Augusta

June 24, 1952

Miss Susan Miles
112 No. Irving Street
San Angelo, Texas

Dear Miss Miles:
   We do not find any information about Lieutenant T. L. Chadbourne, who was killed in the Mexican War.
   We do not have a file of the Eastport Sentinel. As that paper is
still publishing, we are sending your letter there.

Yours very truly,

Marion B. Stubbs

MBS:G

Then apparently she wrote to the Buffalo Historical Society, perhaps hoping that since he had been stationed at Fort
Niagara she would find some trace of the lieutenant there:

THE BUFFALO HISTORICAL SOCIETY
Delaware Park
BUFFALO 7, N.Y.

July 17, 1952

Miss Susan Miles
112 North Irving Street
San Angelo, Texas

Dear Miss Miles:
The following notice of the death of Lieut. T. L. Chadbourne is
from the *Morning Express* of June 1, 1846:

> Lieut. THEODORE LINCOLN CHADBOURNE, who was killed in
> the charge upon the Mexican battery under Capt. MAY, was for-
> merly attached to the garrison at Fort Niagara, and was much
> esteemed by the citizens of this vicinity as an intelligent and ac-
> complished gentleman. He was 24 years old, and graduated at

West Point in 1843. He was a native of Eastport [*sic*] Maine, and a grandson of Gen. LINCOLN.

I found the following additional biographical data in a *List of Officers of the Army of the United States from 1799 to 1900*, compiled from the Official Records by Colonel Wm. H. Powell:

Born in Maine. Appointed at Large. Bvt. 2nd Lieut. 2nd Inf., 1 July, 1843. 2nd Lieut. 8th Inf., 10 Sept., 1845. Killed 9 May, 1846, at the Battle of Resaca de la Palma, Mexico.

If I can be of further service, please let me know.

Very truly yours,

Alice J. Pickup
Librarian

She then heard again from the editor of the *Eastport Sentinel*, who wrote a postcard, undated:

Dear Madam:
Your letter of June 21 addressed to the Maine State Librarian has been forwarded to us. I'll write today to our Register of Probate to see if complete Sentinel files are kept there. If they are not I'm affraid that the records you seek simply are not in existence.
I'm dreadfully sorry that we cannot be of greater assistance to you.

Cordially yours,

/s/ Gerald White

But the register of the probate could offer no help:

PROBATE COURT
County of Washington
Machias, Maine

July Eighteenth, 1952

Mrs. Susan Miles
112 North Irving Street
San Angelo, Texas

Dear Madam:
Mr. Gerald White, Editor of the "Eastport Sentinel" of Eastport, Maine, has written me asking that I contact you relative to copies of the above newspaper which are on file in this Court House.
Mr. White states that you are interested in one Lt. T. L. Chadbourne who was killed in the Mexican War on May 9, 1846. I have checked the copies of the above paper and can find no copies covering the years from 1832 to 1853. I do not know whether the paper

ceased publication during those years, or just why the papers are not on file.

I am sorry that I can give you no further information.

Very truly yours,

Susan M. Dyer, Register

Then Miss Miles heard again from one of her earlier correspondents, Hannah C. Denton:

July 26 [1952]

Dear Miss Miles:

It is a long time since I have heard from you or written you but our correspondence was recalled to me not long ago when one of my sons who lives in Michigan told me of seeing something in the "Times" that might interest you.

There was a notice, he didn't remember in what connection, but in Washington there were items pertaining to the Mexican War, apparently articles that might have belonged to soldiers who fought in the war.

I'm sorry to be so vague about it and now that I've begun to tell you I realize that I should ask him just where these things were to be found. The idea seemed to be that they might be claimed by descendants. I should of course have followed up the matter but I didn't for various reasons, time, etc.

I trust you have been well. I'll write my son and get some more definite information.

Sincerely yours,

Hannah C. Denton

July and August 1952 replies to Miss Miles's letters from Texas sources follow:

THE LIBRARY OF THE UNIVERSITY OF TEXAS

AUSTIN - 12 - TEXAS

July 29, 1952

Miss Susan Miles
112 North Irving Street
San Angelo, Texas

Dear Miss Miles:

Our index to Texas newspapers does not have any citation to the name of T. L. Chadbourne. I have taken your letter on to the newspaper collection, but the librarian is ill; so I'm not sure when they will be able to get around to the checking. There is no biography of Chadbourne for the *Handbook*; so I had no source of information

there. It might be that an inquiry of the Adjutant General's Office
or the National Archives in Washington might get the dope on his
military record.

The enclosed sketch of the Battle of Resaca de la Palma is from
the *Dictionary of American History*. The content comes from Justin
Smith, *The War with Mexico*, Vol. I. If you want the more detailed
account I suggest that you get it photostated, or it is possible that the
Smith book is in the San Angelo Library—or the Junior College
Library. It is a standard work.

I hope that you get results from the newspaper library and from
Texas State Library.

Sincerely yours,

Llerena Friend
Librarian, Barker Texas History Center

TEXAS STATE LIBRARY

TEXAS STATE ARCHIVES

State Highway Building

Austin 11, Texas

August 20, 1952

Miss Susan Miles
112 No. Irving
San Angelo, Texas

Dear Miss Miles:

We have searched our file of the Texas Democrat for 1846 but are
sorry to say that we did not find the account of the battle of Resaca
de la Palma. Our file is not complete.

The Battle is written up in the Encyclopaedia Britannica. You
may have seen this sketch, but we thought to mention it.

Sincerely yours,

Harriet Smither,
State Archivist

HS/br

THE LIBRARY OF THE UNIVERSITY OF TEXAS

AUSTIN - 12 - TEXAS

August 25, 1952

Miss Susan Miles
112 North Irving
San Angelo, Texas

Dear Miss Miles:

I regret my delay in answering your inquiry of July 25 directed
to the Newspaper Collection by Miss Llerena Friend—I have been
away for some time.

Our indexes to newspaper files are rather limited, and provided no specific entries for Lt. T. L. Chadbourne. Our search of what May 1846 files we have turned up no mention. Casualty lists are not complete. I hesitate to send accounts of the battle as they appear in the day by day reports of even a paper with such good correspondence as *The Daily Picayune* (New Orleans). The various reports are not complete in themselves and include a good deal of relatively extraneous material. A concise account of the actions at Palo Alto and Resaca de la Palma can be found in Alfred H. Bill's *Rehearsal for conflict, the war with Mexico, 1846–1848*. You may find that work or similar histories at your public library, or it could be borrowed from here.

Very truly yours,

N. A. Cleveland, Jr.
Librarian, Newspaper Collection

Martha Thompson, the Eastport librarian, wrote again in September regarding photographs of the Chadbourne house; she calls her Irving instead of Miles, taking the street name by mistake:

15 Water St.
Eastport Public Library Association
Eastport, Maine

Sept. 17 - 52

Dear Mrs. Irving:

I hope that you will pardon the delay in not answering your letters. I have been on my vacation and the Library was closed. On returning I found your letter.

I got in touch with Miss Madge Mitt and her sister Mrs. Jessie Ramsy. Miss Mitt admitted that she had heard from you and never answered. She said she had a lot of snap-shots and would send them to you. The house is very lovely with five gardens and is the original Chadbourne home. I also have been told that they have a picture of Lincoln Chadbourne. Dr. Lincoln's wife who lived in Dennysville, Me, was also a relative but died early last spring. I will call again about the snap-shots.

Sincerely,

Martha J. Thompson, Librarian

Miss Miles's marginal note indicates that she received the next item from West Point on March 6, 1963. It identifies General Churchill, who was responsible for getting the cane to the Chadbourne family:

GENERAL ORDERS   WAR DEPARTMENT,

NO. 205.   Adjutant General's Office

Washington, Dec. 12, 1862.

The General-in-Chief announces to the Army the death of Brevet Brigadier General SYLVESTER CHURCHILL, late Inspector General. He died in this city on the 7th instant, at the advanced age of eighty.

General CHURCHILL may well be called a soldier of the Old School. He entered the Army in March, 1812; was retained in the Artillery at the reduction, in 1815; appointed Inspector General in 1841; and was breveted Brigadier General for gallant and meritorious conduct in the battle of Buena Vista, February 23, 1847. Between 1836 and 1841, he was employed as Acting Inspector General in the Creek and Florida wars; and was then commended by the Government for extraordinary vigilance and judgment. He was an exact disciplinarian, and an upright man; and the effect of his discipline and example, while commanding part of the column under General Wool on the march from San Antonio to Monclova, was conspicuous in his troops in the memorable battle which followed soon after, and in which he was personally so distinguished.

He has survived but a brief period the retirement from active service to which he was forced by the infirmities of age; a necessity which his patriotic and martial spirit deplored as coming in the time of his country's need.

In respect to the memory of the deceased, the officers of the Inspector General's Department will wear the usual badge of mourning for thirty days.

BY COMMAND OF MAJOR GENERAL HALLECK:

E. D. TOWNSEND,

Assistant Adjutant General

The personal letters to and from the lieutenant remain. Otherwise, that's the last item I have in the file of Miss Miles's correspondence. I wonder what I missed; I wonder what is lost.

She wanted to know, I guess. She found out a lot, and she named a building and acquired a cane and a book and a sword belt and sword and some letters. She saved him from silence. She saved him for San Angelo and Fort Concho, and for me.

Eleven

Will I Ever Know You?

I hadn't expected letters, not his letters. I had expected only silence, or perhaps the testimony of others. Those who might have said most—classmates and fellow officers who were with him out there—said least, but Miss Miles, through Katharine Waring, reached far beyond herself and showed me his letters.

For a long time I didn't read them. Those I have already shown, please remember, are photostats from federal archives. What remains, what I haven't shown, are originals that Miss Miles acquired from the family. For a long time I didn't read them. Once I knew the letters were there, once I had copies that I could look at whenever I pleased, I wanted to believe that he was there, or perhaps I only wanted to believe that I could find whatever it was that I wanted to find.

Perhaps he's there. Perhaps not. Perhaps I can find him. Perhaps I can't. I'd like to be certain, but I'm not. I do know that once I had copies of the letters in my hand, I felt better. They made a warm place inside me.

I'm pretty certain, sometimes even insistent, about which pipe tobacco I want to smoke and which coffee and white wine I want to drink. I want burley tobacco that's cut coarse. I buy it in bulk at a pipe shop. It's pure tobacco, with none of the additives that some packaged tobaccos and all cigarettes have. About coffee I'm not so particular, so long as it's made strong. The white wine has to be cheap and in a big jug. I prefer Carlo Rossi Rhine Wine, made on the Rhine River, which wanders from Germany through parts of northern California.

But about most other things I'm often uncertain. I sometimes admire—but always at a careful distance—people who seem to have a sure sense of themselves, who are sure in their integrity and judgment. I'm mostly not. Sometimes, I'm not even sure of my own identity. Some people have apparently found me dear enough and easygoing, but others have clearly found me arrogant and domineering. It's little wonder that sometimes I can't find myself at all.

And so when arguments come up, I'm easily unsettled, easily disturbed into doubt. Sometimes I feel strongly both ways as an argument progresses, and sometimes I add a third and a fourth way. It doesn't take much to ruin any calm I've previously achieved. An argument that appears to make sense, even if it contradicts what I thought I had earlier believed, is likely to bring everything into question. I begin to doubt what I had thought, and the first thing you know, everything has come loose.

Such arguments sometimes occur just before I'm supposed to go to class. There I am, trying to be wise, or at least serene, or at least competent as I head for class, and someone reminds me that things may be otherwise than I think. Or maybe I read something that tells me I've got it all wrong. What am I to do? Go on to class and get it all wrong there, too? Then go to class another time and say everything in an altogether different way? That sometimes happens.

All of us have been, knowingly or not, part of a rhetorical tradition that has been with us for 2,500 years. This tradition allowed and encouraged us to believe that we could achieve identity not just in what we do but also in what we say and write, and that others could know us in what we say and write, and that they could tell themselves back to us in their words. That tradition—it goes back to Aristotle and before—still predicts, influences, and guides much of what happens in composition classes throughout our schools.

In that old tradition, we believed or wanted to believe that the author was in the text that he or she wrote, making a self known to the reader who approached. Aristotle says in his *Rhetoric* that ethos is potent, that ethical argument is more persuasive than logical argument or emotional appeal. *Ethos,* as he and others since have used the term, means character, the character of the speaker or writer, as it is revealed in the text—not as it was known previously, but as it emerges in speech and writing. Ethical argument, then, is argument that rests upon the revealed ethos, or character. Something like that is what I've been waiting to read in the work of composition students.

I have wanted student writers to show themselves to me in what they write, to give themselves to me, as I try to show and to give myself back to them in what I write. I have wanted them to remember their lives, their histories, the particularities of their existence, and to show them to me. I have wanted to know what they think and how they think and why they think that way, and I have wanted to know the particular experiences that counted to them. I have wanted them to cherish themselves at least enough to remember and to understand who and what they are. I have wanted them to cherish what they write and to believe that I cherish them as authors. I want us all to be there, present to each other. I wish we could all be here forever, each of us cherished. I had hoped that it would someday be possible.

But that's on Monday in my freshman composition class. On Tuesday, I have to go to my senior literature class, and the confusion and uncertainty begin again. Something altogether otherwise happens there.

When I go to my literature class on Tuesday, I'm obliged to listen to writers of our time who tell me that I've been wrong, who tell me that the old rhetorical tradition never had things quite right. What they say is compelling. I begin to listen and to doubt what I thought I formerly thought. They tell me, and make sense doing so, that I cannot know the author in his or her text. I can only know my interpretation of the author. In *Image, Music, Text*, Roland Barthes remarks that "the birth of the reader must be at cost of the death of the author." And besides, they tell me, the author is not who I think, not some solitary self single-handedly creating a text. The author is a social construction, always a crowd. Stanley Fish says in *Is There a Text in This Class?* that "selves are constituted by the ways of thinking and seeing that inhere in social organizations." If ethos exists, it exists in the perceiving minds of readers. It is not the creation of the solitary author; it is what the community has already made possible and what readers find in the text or project upon the text. The solitary author is dead. Language writes us rather than the other way around; we write what the language of our community will let us write. The notion of the self as a source of meaning, they tell me, is outdated and was always wrong, or at least more complicated than we thought. The language by which we view and construct the world comes from society, not from the individual, who is already gone and was never there. If there is character, it is character found and granted by readers as they respond to a text.

Confusion begins, and uncertainty comes. I wonder what I'm to do when I go back to my composition class on Wednesday. I begin to be afraid that I don't exist. I can't turn away from what I've learned from my literature class, and I don't want to, for it's often exhilarating and provocative. I can't deny the power of the reader to determine the meaning of the text. *Gulliver's Travels* is mine. Sometimes I don't allow it to be Swift's property. I can't deny what some call social constructionist and intertextual thought. It challenges the habits that we sometimes call thoughts and reminds us—for we need to be reminded—that reality is what we have decided to call reality, that facts and logic are what some community has decided they are, that a self exists only in and through the community's interpretation.

Such thoughts leave me lonely. Will no one find me if I manage to say or to write something? Later, will all forget that I was here, or never notice? I had decided that the text of what I wrote was just about all there is to me, but the me that's there is not myself, only some self created out there by others, if they happen to notice. Has Lieutenant Chadbourne vanished before he arrived?

I've wanted to be real in what I wrote, but I have sometimes dodged and juked and hidden, perhaps afraid of what might be revealed, perhaps intent on believing that there's more to me than a reader can find. Perhaps, after all, I don't exist even in my own little text. I can't keep things sorted out. They won't stay in tidy files or neat compartments for me. What they say is true in literary theory slops over into everything else, and I begin to go fuzzy around the edges, on my way toward disappearance. A colleague tries to reassure me. "Now, now," he says, "it's going to be all right. When Barthes says that the author dies, he doesn't mean the *person* dies." He pats me on the shoulder. "How do you keep them separate?" I ask, but he doesn't answer.

If the author of an essay or a poem in the literature anthology is dead to me, if I can never find him or her, must I learn that I will never find my composition students either? Has Lieutenant Chadbourne vanished before he arrived?

I don't think so, but I'm a little uncertain. Things usually aren't all one way or another.

Sometimes I can remember what I might have remembered all along. Everything anyone ever wrote intrudes upon, alters, blesses, and damns anything anyone else writes. The language doesn't belong to any one of us.

Still, I think I'm here, though I'm a little uncertain. I think you may be here. I think composition students may be here. A little while back, I said that "I'm obliged to listen to writers of our time who tell me that I've been wrong." What obliges me? I'm obliged because they're compelling. They pull at me. They are real.

If they are real, there's a chance that I might be, too, some day. Lieutenant Chadbourne may yet emerge in the letters that are waiting, altogether accountable for himself.

Twelve

West Point

W hat his letters tell of his life will have to wait. They are their own story. I can tell a little, but not much: twenty-three years doesn't give a fellow much time to get into history, or into history books.

His family, I assume, sometimes called him Link, for he signed some of his letters so. He was born in Eastport, Maine, on August 2, 1822, to Hannah Lincoln Chadbourne and Ichabod Rollins Chadbourne. The family had been in New England, apparently, since 1631.

William Chadbourne, the family genealogy says, probably came from Devonshire with James Wall and John Goddard, all carpenters, in a vessel called the *Pied Cow*, which landed on July 8, 1632, at a place still called Cow's Cove. They had come to work for John Mason, and they built the first sawmill in New England.

But he wasn't the first. His son, Humphrey, was already here, had come in the *Warwick*, landing September 9, 1631. He came as chief carpenter for David Thompson, patenter, and built what was called the "Great House of Strawberry Bank," a blockhouse for defense against the Indians in what is now Portsmouth, Maine. Thomas Bailey Aldrich, in *An Old Town by the Sea*, says that "Mr Humphrey Chadbourne consciously or unconsciously sowed the seed from which a city has sprung." On May 10, 1643, he bought a large tract of land from the Indians in Newichawannock. Since the family genealogy reports that the land remained in the family for over two hundred years, I assume that it is the place, later Eastport, where Link Chadbourne was born. Humphrey Chadbourne was active in Kittery town affairs. He was a selectman, an officer of militia, town clerk, deputy to the General Court, and associate judge of York County. Sarah Orne Jewett refers to him as "the lawgiver of Kittery."

Humphrey's son, another Humphrey, born in 1653, married Sarah Bolles of Walls and Cape Porpoise.

Their son William, born in 1683, married Mary, whose last name neither the genealogy nor I know.

Their son Benjamin was born in Berwick, Maine, on July 23, 1718. On July 21, 1742, he married Sarah Heard. I assume that she died, for on October 10, 1751, he married Mary Chesley, of Durham, New Hampshire. I quote the genealogy. Benjamin

> served as capt. in Col. Jonathan Bergley's regiment of Louisberg, 1745. Was attorney and counselor at law. Colonel in militia. Judge of Court of Common Pleas. Representative to General Court from Berwick for 15 years, 1756–1771. Member of Governor's Council 1780–1784. One of the founders of Berwick Academy established in 1791. For the academy he gave ten acres of land in the finest possible situation and a sum of money to begin the subscription. Rev. John Lord, D.D., in his historical address on Berwick Academy refers to Judge Chadbourne as a "veritable patrician with a great landed estate which his ancestors purchased from the Indians. He lived in a fine colonial mansion surrounded by noble elms. He sent to John Hancock a large number of elms from his Berwick estate to be planted on Boston Common where some still exist." When his house was built, there was no house between it and Canada. Sarah Orne Jewitt has made Judge Chadbourne one of the characters in her historical romance "The Tory Lover," picturing him as "an old man of singular dignity and kindliness of look."

Benjamin Chadbourne and Sarah Heard had four children, all lost to me in silence and oblivion. He and Mary Chesley had four children. One of them was Ichabod Rollins Chadbourne, born in 1787 in South Berwick, Maine, a graduate of Dartmouth in 1808, a lawyer at Eastport, Maine, and the father of Lieutenant Chadbourne. Ichabod Rollins Chadbourne married Dolly Dana of Eastport, Maine, in 1818. On October 21, 1821, he married Hannah Lincoln, daughter of Theodore and

Hannah Mayhew Lincoln of Dennysville, Maine. Their children were the following:

> Theodore Lincoln, August 1, 1822–May 9, 1846 [*Note:* the genealogy says August 1, not August 2.]
> George Wallingford, February 19, 1824–November 15, 1871
> Benjamin Lincoln, April 30, 1826
> Hannah Lincoln, March 18, 1828
> Alexander Scammel, July 7, 1830
> Elizabeth Rollins, July 9, 1832–November 17, 1850
> Bela Lincoln, October 9, 1834–April 7, 1848
> Edmund Lincoln, April 28, 1838–November 7, 1839
> Thomas Lincoln, April 13, 1841

The first died at Resaca de la Palma. Three others died young. From the descendants of the others Susan Miles acquired a book, a sword, a sword belt, and some letters.

I have trusted the genealogy. Through it, I know as much about some of Lieutenant Chadbourne's ancestors as I know about his early life.

Truth is, I know nothing about his early life.

Perhaps if I went to Eastport, I'd somehow learn. I don't have the time, strength, or money to go to Eastport. Let go of me for a little, Lieutenant Chadbourne, let go.

Still, if I'd paid attention to Eastport earlier, and to a letter I couldn't read, I might sooner have guessed at a connection to Link Chadbourne's boyhood. According to the 1937 *Maine, a Guide 'Down East,'* written by workers of the WPA's Federal Writers' Project, Eastport in the 1930s had a population of a little over 3,400. For a long time the town was important for the cod, haddock, cusk, hake, pollock, halibut, and herring brought in there, but its importance had long since waned before *Maine* was written. The town was settled in 1780, though European traders were there earlier. Fort Sullivan was established there in 1808 for the protection of the settlers, but the British captured the town anyway in July 1814. Fort Sullivan was on a high ledge behind what would in the 1930s be Shead Memorial High School.

The indecipherable letter I referred to earlier—it was photocopied and a part of Susan Miles's collection—was mailed

to Lieutenant Chadbourne's parents with a gift from Brigadier General Sylvester Churchill. The gift he sent them was a
walking stick made from a tree that had been shattered by a
cannonball on the battlefield of Resaca de la Palma. Churchill,
already inspector general of the army, distinguished himself in
Mexico, especially at Buena Vista.

And it seems entirely likely that he already knew the Chadbourne family. David C. Hensley's *Brigadier General Sylvester
Churchill* reports that at least in 1835 he was the commanding officer at Fort Sullivan. Eastport couldn't have been much
more populous in 1835 than it was in the 1930s, and it might
have been considerably smaller. I'd guess that the fort commandant, Churchill, probably knew Ichabod Chadbourne, who
was a notable man in the town.

Maybe, too, there was another connection. General Churchill's son, William Hunter Churchill, must have been about
three years older than Link Chadbourne. He went to West
Point in 1836 and graduated, eighth in his class, in 1840. He
was assigned to artillery and served in the Florida Indian Wars,
1840–42. He won a brevet in Mexico. He was wounded at Palo
Alto on the day before the battle of Resaca de la Palma and
never recovered: he died at Point Isabel on October 19, 1847.
Maybe they knew each other.

From his letters I can tell a little about what life at West
Point was like for him, but his letters must wait. They are their
own story. But even without his letters I can guess a little about
what life there was like for him.

He went to West Point when he was barely seventeen. The
second volume of *The Centennial of the United States Military Academy at West Point* lists thirteen publications of lithographs, engravings, drawings, and watercolor sketches done
between 1834 and 1841 of scenes at or near West Point. One
of them is a lithograph of a summer encampment, now hang-
ing in the academy library, done by Seth Eastman, class of
1829, who would later serve at Fort Chadbourne. An enter-
prising searcher might from these get glimpses of what Cadet
Chadbourne saw when he went to the academy in 1839. J. H.
Colton's *Guide Book to West Point and Vicinity; Containing
Descriptive, Historical, and Statistical Sketches of the United
States Military Academy, and of Other Subjects of Interest*, pub-

lished in 1844, also provides a little testimony about the setting. Colton remarks of himself in his preface that, "being
Unconnected with the Military Academy, and having no partial interests to serve, the writer wishes to be regarded simply
as a 'looker on in Venice.'" Not everyone was without partial interests. The Military Academy had for some years come
under severe attack. Stephen E. Ambrose recounts the attacks
in *Duty, Honor, Country, a History of West Point*, and Joseph B.
James cites the troubles more briefly (in "Life at West Point
One Hundred Years Ago," *Mississippi Valley Historical Review*,
June 1944):

> The leveling tendencies of the new democracy that rode the wave
> of westward expansion caused graduates of the United States Mili-
> tary Academy to be derided as "puppets and aristocrats." Repre-
> sentatives of the people expressed in Congress the contempt of their
> constituents and proceeded to bait both the regular army and the
> Academy.
>
> This attitude, coupled with the traditional American prejudice
> against standing armies, is further reflected in congressional agita-
> tion to reduce the size of the army, already less than six thousand
> men scattered in a hundred posts. The conflict between the admin-
> istration of John Tyler and the adherents of Henry Clay, in addition
> to the usual interparty strife between Whigs and Democrats, caused
> this issue to become a veritable political football.

"The sources, from which these materials have been derived,"
Colton says, "are various":

> Much, of course, is the result of observation. Congressional docu-
> ments and other papers, not easy of reference, have been examined,
> and have contributed somewhat to the contents. Other works have
> been consulted, and when necessary quoted, and diligent care has
> been taken to have every statement correct.

I linger over Colton's *Guide Book*: Lieutenant Chadbourne
has not told me what he saw and did. Colton begins with his
own arrival:

> In landing at West Point the first thing attracting attention is the
> perfect order and regularity that prevail. There is no tumult, no
> boisterous shout, and no annoying crowd. All is quiet and decorum.
>
> A guard is stationed at the wharf, and it was formerly the custom
> to take the names of all gentlemen arriving at and leaving the post,
> in order that the commandant might be immediately informed of

the arrival and departure of visitors and officers. It happens not in-
frequently that an officer of distinction is received with a salute and
with other military honors suited to his rank.

An omnibus, Colton reports, is available to take passengers to
the hotel or to other destinations, but many send their luggage
up and climb the hill on foot, either by the road or by "a more
direct foot-path which goes immediately up the hill."

> The hotel, though at some considerable distance from any other
> building, occupies perhaps the finest situation on the plain. It stands
> at an elevation of about one hundred and sixty feet, upon the brow
> of the hill, overlooking the river. Around it extends a large plain, in
> the north-east corner of which are the ruins of Fort Clinton. Near
> these is the encampment ground, where the cadets spend eight or
> ten weeks of the summer in their tents. The south side of the plain
> is bounded by the most important public buildings, and on the west
> are located the residences of the superintendent and other offi-
> cers. The nearest of the chain of hills encircling the plain is Mount
> Independence, which rises in majestic grandeur, bearing upon its
> summit the crumbling masonry of Fort Putnam.
>
> Above West Point, the river forms, apparently, a beautiful lake,
> at the northern extremity of which, some eight miles distant, stands
> the goodly town of Newburgh. The whole distance is enlivened and
> beautified with the sails of numerous vessels, while on either side
> are steep and lofty hills, forming the doorposts, as it were, of this
> broad avenue. On the side hill, west of the hotel, is seen the Ar-
> tillery Laboratory, a stone building with turrets and battlements,
> presenting a warlike appearance, though on a small scale. . . .
>
> After this general description of the view from the hotel, it is our
> purpose to notice more particularly the walks and buildings in the
> vicinity . . .

Colton's later, more particular, notes tell of his passing "the
buildings occupied by some of the officers of the Institution, with gardens adjoining them, the arrangement of which
evinces much taste." Then, he reports, "we turn suddenly to
the left, around the Mess Hall of the Cadets, a low building,
not remarkable in its appearance." A nearby lot has been
reserved for the erection of new barracks, "whenever Congress
may make appropriations sufficient for their erection."

> The South Barrack is the next building on the left, and at right
> angles to this stands the North Barrack. The former has been built
> about thirty years, and is very poorly adapted to the necessities of

the Institution. Its construction is such as to expose its inmates to great inconveniences, and to sickness; and both of the buildings occupy a part of the plain which should be laid open for military operations. It will add much to the advantage of the Institution and to the appearance of the place, if these two buildings and the Mess Hall are removed from their present localities, and a new building is erected, sufficient to contain all the Cadets, better adapted to the preservation of a strict police, with proper apparatus for warmth and ventilation, and in a style of architecture suited to modern views of improvement.

Colton's recommended walking tour next takes him by the principal classroom building, the Academy, a "commodious stone edifice, 275 feet long, and 75 feet broad, with three stories and a basement." It was completed in 1838, just in time for Lieutenant Chadbourne. Then he locates the road to the hospital, passes the Chapel, the Philosophical and Library building, "with a dome and mural towers for astronomical observations," goes on to Kosciuszko's Garden, by a battery on the riverbank, and up through the ruins of Fort Clinton and to Kosciuszko's monument.

"The stranger at West Point," Colton advises later, "will find it pleasant to witness such military displays as are made from time to time":

> The daily morning parade at 8 a.m., during the encampment, and the evening parade at sunset, are ceremonies in which the whole corps of Cadets participate. The morning parade is followed by the guard mounting, and beside these exercises, there are daily drills in artillery, infantry or cavalry tactics, occurring at various hours. Occasionally the day is devoted to a review of the Cadets in the presence of strangers of military rank.

In the evening, three times a week, the excellent band connected with the corps, are stationed on the plain to play for the benefit of all who choose to listen. The music is of the first order, and is well regarded as one of the chief attractions of the place. In the winter concerts are sometimes given by a full orchestra.

The cadets, Colton reports, have dancing parties in the Academy during the summer, "to which very general invitations are given," and one or two balls during the encampment. In *Duty, Honor, Country*, Ambrose remarks:

> Summer was the social season, as girls went to the Point from the South and New York City to escape the heat. Hops and balls marked the weekends, and a dancing master was available to give lessons, at 2.00 a month, to those cadets who wanted them. The season began on July 4, with the climax coming at the end of encampment, when a grand ball was held. The dancing began at nine, and the four hundred people present wheeled back and forth to the cotillion, Spanish dances, galopades, and waltzes. At midnight refreshments, "consisting of all the luxuries which New York could afford," were served. Then the dances resumed, to continue until four in the morning.

The luxuries of New York were reported by Cadet James Wall Schureman, class of 1842, in a letter to his sister. He won a brevet in Mexico and died in California on January 30, 1852, at age thirty. Colton also tells about another entertainment during the summer encampment, the *stag dance*, performed in the open air:

> Large numbers of candles are placed on the ground, in two rows, several feet apart. The space between is occupied by the dancers, who move to the sound of fife and drum, or of the violin, in regular time, but with every variety of posture. The ludicrous positions assumed, and the enthusiasm manifested in the sport attract crowds of spectators, who are greatly diverted with the entertainment. At the sound of tattoo, the lights are suddenly extinguished, and in a few moments the place is completely deserted.

But there are no literary exhibitions, Colton says, "nor is there at present among them any literary society for improvement in debate and composition."

The library, Colton notes, "has its ceiling beautifully ornamented with architectural designs. Full-length portraits of

Jefferson and of Madison, both by Sully, hang on the walls, and in the recess for the librarian's desk, there is a bust of Washington. The stained windows add to the beauty of the room. The library is open from 8:00 to 12:00 A.M. and from 1:00 P.M. until sundown.

> Only the members of the Institution and officers residing at the post are allowed to take books from the Library, but citizens have access to it, at the regular hours, with liberty to examine such books as they please. Cadets are allowed on Saturday afternoons to take any books they may have been reading during the week, to be returned on the following Monday; at other times they may have a single volume of any work calculated to aid them in their studies.

According to Colton's report, the library holds 14,564 volumes, of which 3,654 are duplicates. "Of the present character of the library," Colton says, the following may convey some idea: on military engineering, 2,327 volumes, of which 2,090 are duplicates; on artillery and pyrotechny, 508 volumes, of which 346 are duplicates; on military art, 692 volumes, with 149 duplicates; on military history, memoirs, and campaigns, 876 volumes, with 94 duplicates; on civil engineering, 638 volumes, with 36 duplicates; on mathematics, 969 volumes, with 322 duplicates; on chemistry, mineralogy, geology, natural history, the arts, and medicine, 1,645 volumes, with 53 duplicates; on history, biography, memoirs, and travel, 2,518 volumes, with 190 duplicates; and in miscellaneous literature, 3,081 volumes, with 145 duplicates. Reactions to the library varied according to the background and previous education of the cadets. As Ambrose puts it:

> Some thought it excellent, some denounced it as ridiculously poor. Ulysses Grant [class of 1843], a tanner's son, was impressed by the library, while Henry A. du Pont [class of 1861], after a few unsuccessful ventures, never bothered to visit it. James Harrison Wilson [class of 1860] came from an Illinois family with some pretensions to culture and thus represented something of a middle ground. He thought the twenty-thousand volumes in the library were good enough as far as they went but that the orientation was too heavily military and foreign.

The Academy was the setting for the cadets' classroom and laboratory work and study:

The first story contains a large room used for a riding hall and for military exercises during the winter. The apartment at the north end is occupied as a fencing hall, and the corresponding one at the other end is the court room. In the second story are a number of recitation rooms, the Quarter-master's and Treasurer's offices, and the Engineering room. The latter, an apartment 75 by 22, is furnished with numerous models to illustrate the important branches of architecture, fortification, and civil engineering. Most conspicuous in this room are two large models of English manufacture, one of which represents a perfect fortification in all its minutiae, displaying the proper construction of the walls, and the means of protecting the various avenues of approach. The other represents the progress of a successful attack upon a fortification. The advancing army, in miniature, are represented as having passed barrier after barrier, driving the besieged before them. In one place they have made a breach in the walls by the explosion of a mine, and in another they have raised a mound to protect themselves in their advance. The besieged have retreated to their last barrier, and are making preparations, in case that should be taken, to retreat to the buildings of the town, part of which is in ruins. As their last resort they are fortifying a church, which has already suffered some injury. These models, interesting simply as curiosities, must be of great importance in illustrating the nature and defence of fortifications.

The room, Colton reports, also has models of the most celebrated Grecian temples and of bridges, canal locks, steam engines, waterwheels, and arches. On the third story above the Engineering Room is what Colton calls the Mineralogical Cabinet, "a well selected and well arranged collection of the most important specimens of native and foreign minerals, embracing some of considerable value." The Drawing Hall is at the opposite end of the third floor; it is "supplied with every necessary convenience for drawing and painting." Also on the third floor are a sculpture gallery and a painting gallery. The painting gallery

> contains a few pieces from foreign artists, and some engravings, designed as lessons to be copied: but it is intended that the walls shall be chiefly covered with the best of the paintings produced by the Cadets. Each year the teacher selects such as he deems most worthy of preservation, and allows the Cadets to retain the remainder. A stimulus to exertion is thus held out to them, and at the same

time the Academy reaps some immediate benefit from their labors. A large number of paintings has already been collected, and their appearance would do credit to more advanced artists.

Colton's *Guide Book* tells, too, how the academy is administered, relying chiefly on *Regulations for the Military Academy, by the President of the United States* (1839). Candidates selected by the War Department, we learn, "are required to report themselves for examination to the Superintendent of the Academy between the 1st and 20th of June, annually. The only requisite attainments are the ability to read and write well, and a knowledge of the elements of arithmetic, including reduction, proportion, and fractions."

I am assuming that since Colton's *Guide Book* was published in 1844, his visit to West Point and his study of appropriate resources more than likely occurred during the time that Lieutenant Chadbourne was a cadet. The course of studies at that time, Colton says, was as follows (I am summarizing, not quoting):

Infantry tactics: includes drill of the soldier, company, and battalion, evolutions of the line, the manual exercise of light infantry and riflemen, and police of camp and garrison.

Mathematics: includes algebra, geometry, trigonometry, mensuration, descriptive and analytical geometry, and fluxions.

French language: includes French grammar, accurate translations, and correct pronunciation; French was included in the curriculum not just for the sake of polite usage in polite society but also for the sake of access to major treatises in military science and tactics, which, it was assumed, would mostly be written in French.

Drawing: includes the elements of the human figure, elementary studies in landscape with the pencil, shading and finishing, landscape in India ink, and elements of topography with pen, pencil, India ink, and colors.

Natural and experimental philosophy: includes mechanics, magnetism, and astronomy.

Chemistry: includes chemical philosophy, application of chemistry to the arts, mineralogy, and geology.

Artillery: includes nomenclature and description of various kinds and parts of artillery, exercise with fieldpieces, maneuvers as a division of artillery, gunnery theory and practice, pyrotechny, and preparation of powder, rockets, and fireballs.

Engineering: includes civil engineering, field fortification, permanent fortification, and the science of war.

History: includes English grammar, rhetoric, geography, ancient history and sword exercise of cavalry.

This course of study lasted four years. The oldest class is called the *first*, the next the *second*, and so on. "In the months of July and August the Cadets are encamped, and the instruction is exclusively military," though there was time, for example, for dancing lessons. Colton includes a chart showing how the curriculum given above was organized over the four years.

What has been designed for everyone, I am assuming, will reach every one. Link Chadbourne, I expect, went through the course of study I've shown, and I expect that everything else that applied to all also applied to him.

Annual examinations, for example. These were held in January and in June, "at which time all the Cadets are examined by the Academic Board (consisting of the superintendent, professors, and teachers) in the presence of a Board of Visitors, who are army officers, designated for the purpose by the Secretary of War, who sometimes attends in person." Former superintendent Thayer's regimen was still intact in Link Chadbourne's time at West Point, and it had been Thayer's intention that every student would perform in every subject every day. Cadets were expected to come to the classroom with a thorough knowledge of the day's lesson and to be ready to go to the blackboard and discuss any part of the lesson thoroughly. Since they were graded on each day's performance, cadets could not neglect their work and then study intensively for the finals in January and June. The cadets, according to Ambrose, approached finals in trepidation, took them in nervousness, and finished them in relief. After the June examinations in 1854, Cadet Edward L. Hartz, class of 1855, wrote to his father (as Ambrose reports):

"I write with a feeling of exultation and true gratification. I have passed the second class June examination upon the most extended and difficult course of philosophy, comprising mechanics, acoustics, Optics, astronomy and magnetism taught at any institution in the world." Questions might be either general or specific, and

Synopsis of the Course of Studies at the U.S. Military Academy—June 1844.

	Department	Instructors	Text Books, Etc.
First Class	Engineering, and Science of War	Prof. Mahan, Lieut. Wright, Lieut. Newton, Lieut. Rosecrans	Military Engineering—Treatise on Field Fortification. do Lithographic Notes on Permanent Fortification, Attack and Defence, Mines and other accessories, Composition of Armies, Strategy, &c. Civil Engineering—Course of Civil Engineering. Lithographic Notes on Architecture, Stone Cutting and Machines.
	Ethics	Prof. Parks, Lieut. Scammon	Blair's Rhetoric. Wayland's Elements of Moral Science, abridged. Kent's Commentaries. Hedge's Elements of Logic.
	Infantry Tactics	Capt. Thomas	Rules and Regulations for the Exercise and Maneuvres of the United States' Infantry.
	Artillery	Lieut. Knowlton	U. S. Artillery Tactics. Kinsley's Pyrotechny. Thiroux's Instruction Theoretique et Practique d'Artillerie. Knowlton's Notes on Gunpowder, Percussion Powder, Cannon and Projectiles.
	Mineralogy and Geology	Prof. Bailey, Lieut. Kendrick	Dana's Mineralogy. Hitchcock's Geology.

Class	Subject	Instructors	Text-Books
Second Class	Natural and Experimental Philosophy	Prof. Bartlett, Lieut. Roberts, Lieut. Gilham	Courtenay's Beauchariat's Traité de Mechanique. Rochet's Electricity and Magnetism. Bartlett's Optics. Gummere's Astronomy.
	Chemistry	Prof. Bailey, Lieut. Kendrick	Kane's Chemistry.
	Drawing	Mr. Weir, and Lieut. R. S. Smith	Landscape. Topography.
Third Class	Mathematics	Prof. Church, Lieut. Vogdes, Bvt. Capt. Hanson, Lieut. Howe, Lieut. Stewart	Davies' Shades, Shadows, and Perspective. Davies' Spherical Projections and Warped Surfaces. Davies' Surveying. Davies' Analytical Geometry. Church's Calculus.
	French Language	Mr. Berard, Mr. Agnel, Lieut. D'Orémieulx	Bérard's Leçons Françaises. Voyage du Jeune Anacharsis. Murray's English Reader.
	Drawing	Mr. Weir, and Lieut. R. S. Smith	Human Figure. Topography.
	English Grammar	Prof. Parks, Lieut. Scammon, Lieut. Johnston.	Willett's Geography and Atlas. Kirkham's Grammar.
Fourth Class	Mathematics	Lieut. Vogdes, Lieut. Clarke, Lieut. H. A. Allen	Davies' Bourdon's Algebra. Davies' Legendre's Geometry and Trigonometry. Davies' Descriptive Geometry.
	French Language	Mr. Berard, Mr. Agnel, Lieut. D'Orémieulx	Lévizac's Grammar. Bérard's Leçons Françaises. Voyage du Jeune Ancharsis.

they ranged over the entire area of the course. One cadet was required to discuss the subject of friction, give its laws, and find a value for the coefficient of friction by means of the inclined plane. Another mathematics question was to prove that the logarithyms of the same numbers in different systems are to each other as the moduli of those systems. In natural philosophy, Cadet Hartz was asked to draw a cross section of the human eye and to explain its construction and the optical principles upon which its efficiency depended. In his final examination of his First Class year, Hartz was required to "show the method of constructing a Crown work for the defence of a bridge head and to show the dispositions which would be made to secure the passage of the river to a large army in the face of the Enemy," and to demonstrate the proper positions of the flankers and rear guards in a march. In ethics he had to discuss the subject of "justice as it respects reputation, and the moral law applicable thereto"; in mineralogy, to give an account of the formation of coral reefs and peat moss "and the agencies which have led to the consolidation of loose material on the surface of the earth." He also took examinations in artillery, infantry, and cavalry tactics.

The summer encampment was generally devoted to practical soldiering. First-class cadets did fieldwork in artillery and engineering. In 1839, the first instruction in horsemanship began. The best horse of Link Chadbourne's day was York, a big chestnut with a strong will. Apparently he didn't tolerate inferior riders; stories indicate that he would throw them and then continue the drill alone. The same stories indicate that York's best rider was Ulysses Grant, who had a way with horses, if not with politics. The chief instructor in military science and tactics, whether in class or in the field, was still Mahan, who taught civil and military engineering and the science of war. Still, perhaps it wasn't enough. In his *Frontiersmen in Blue*, Robert Utley says that the academy

> did not teach a prospective officer how to fight Indians. The incisive lectures of old Professor Dennis Hart Mahan probed the nature and art of war and laid down the principles by which his students would conduct the coming Civil War, but his teachings remained barren of guidance on how to employ a company of dragoons against the only enemy any of them could see in their future. West Point . . . sent them forth to learn Indian fighting by hard experience.

Others have echoed the charge; James L. Morrison does in *The Best School in the World*, though he also argues that Mahan did all he could.

Grades were not held private. A record was kept of every recitation on a scale of merit from 3 to 0, and these were publicly exhibited. After the June examination these records were condensed into rolls displaying the comparative standing of each cadet in his class. These were published in the annual register. The ranking system was often criticized. Opponents said that under the ranking system, cadets near the top studied hard in order to get into the army unit they preferred, cadets near the bottom studied hard in order to stay in school, but cadets in the middle sometimes saw little need to study, for they were bound for the infantry no matter what. Grant, for example, was in the middle, and his memoirs indicate that he seldom looked at a lesson more than once. Morrison, in *The Best School in the World*, suggests that at any rate the ranking system did not correlate with later military success. Grant, Sherman, Sheridan, and Stonewall Jackson, for example, graduated as privates at West Point. The register also contained a *conduct-roll* compiled from a record of all the irregularities and violations of the code of discipline for the year preceding. Offenses were classed "in seven grades of criminality, bringing from 1 to 10 demerits." Absence from reveille rollcall, for example, was 3 demerits; "introducing spiritous liquors into barracks" was 8; and disobedience of orders was 8. For each year after the first, offenses counted more; for a 3-demerit offense, a senior would get 4½. If any cadet accumulated more than 200 demerits in a single year, he was recommended to the War Department for discharge.

During their four years at the academy, cadets were allowed to be absent only once, usually during July and August after their second year. Once they had graduated, they were "connected with the army as second lieutenants, or when there were no vacancies, as brevet second lieutenants." I judge that the *Guide Book* echoes contemporary belief: "After joining any particular regiment, however, they are certain of a liberal support, and of promotion as vacancies occur above them." If that was accepted belief at the time, it's unsurprising that Brevet

Second Lieutenant Chadbourne would have been more than a
little mad when a civilian was appointed ahead of him.

But the *Guide Book* tells more. I learn, for example, that
commissioned officers on the faculty wore the uniforms "of
their several regiments."

> The Cadets have a gray cloth coatee, with standing collar, single
> breasted, having black silk cord, and three rows of gilt bullet
> buttons in front, and also upon the skirts and sleeves; gray cloth
> trowsers for winter, with a black stripe an inch wide down the outer
> seam; white drilling trowsers for summer; white gloves; a dress cap
> of black felt seven inches high, with a black pompon eight inches
> long, a leather cockade, and a gilt castle and eagle on front; a for-
> age cap is worn when not on duty. Each Cadet must unite with his
> room-mate in purchasing the tables and other furniture that may
> be prescribed for their room. No article of clothing, furniture, or
> books can be sold or otherwise disposed of without permission from
> the superintendent.

Pictures often make the uniforms look a little better than they
probably were—usually "ill fitting and always constraining,"
Ambrose says. The coat in particular was celebrated in a cadet
verse:

> Your coat is made, you button it, give one spasmodic cough,
> And do not draw another breath until you take it off.

I learn, too, that the possible punishments for a cadet were
in three classes:

> 1st. Privation of recreation; extra tours of guard duty; reprimands;
> arrests or confinement to his room or tent.

> 2d. Confinement in light prison; confinement in dark prison.

> 3d. Dismission with the privilege of resigning; public dismission.

Any disobedience or disrespectful conduct toward teachers or
officers made a cadet liable to dismissal, and further:

> Cadets are *forbidden* to have or to use intoxicating drinks, tobacco,
> or cards. The following things are prohibited under severe penal-
> ties: all cooking in barracks or in camp; damaging or selling public
> property; absence from quarters, and visiting in study hours, and
> at night; answering for another at roll call; encouraging or provok-

ing duels, ungentlemanly conduct; combinations against authority; publishing accounts of the Academy, or of transactions in the Institution; receiving money or supplies from home; absence from duty; neglect of study; disregard of the Sabbath; profanity; taking a newspaper without permission; having other dress than that prescribed; lending accoutrements; throwing anything from the windows and doors in barracks; having a light burning after 10 p.m.; running, loud talking, and scuffling in barracks; receiving strangers in barracks in study hours.

From surviving reports, the ban did not do much to diminish smoking and drinking among the cadets. The cadets were not allowed to pass over the road surrounding the Plain except on Saturday afternoons, and then only with special permission, and they could not visit with family, except on Saturday afternoons, without special permission.

Each cadet received a monthly allowance of twenty-eight dollars. About ten dollars was needed to pay board. The rest was placed to the cadet's credit or might be used for clothing, books, and furniture. However, two dollars was held back from each month's allowance "for the accumulation of a fund to be applied at the time of his promotion to the purchase of a uniform."

The cadets were organized into four military companies entirely distinct from the four academic classes. The captains and lieutenants were usually drawn from the first class, sergeants from the second class, and corporals from the third class. Four chevrons of single lace on each arm, points up, above the elbow designated the rank of captain, three designated lieutenant, two designated sergeant, and two below the elbow designated corporal.

Cadet rooms in Link Chadbourne's time cannot have been entirely pleasant:

> The buildings at present in use are inconvenient and uncomfortable; they contain but 96 rooms for the accommodation of 237 Cadets, and the consequence is that from two to five persons are crowded into one apartment, which must answer the purposes of a sitting room, bed room, and study. The rooms in the south barrack, about 12 feet square, are scarcely sufficient for one individual, and have the disadvantage of opening directly into the open air. They

are said to be cold and comfortless in winter, and badly ventilated in summer.

Finally, though I have not exhausted the *Guide Book*, I learn the cadets' daily schedule:

5:00 A.M.	reveille
(6:00 A.M. in winter)	roll call
	cleaning of arms and accoutrements
	inspection
	study
7:00 A.M.	breakfast
7:30 A.M.	troop and guard mounting
8:00 A.M. (in summer)	morning parade
(in winter)	study and recitation
	until 1:00 P.M.
1:00 P.M.	dinner
	recreation
2:00–4:00 P.M.	study and recitation
After 4:00 P.M.	military exercises
	recreation
Sunset	evening parade, supper immediately after call to quarters 30 minutes after supper study until 9:30
9:30 P.M.	tattoo
10:00 P.M.	taps
	lights extinguished
	inspection

The schedule was, of course, different during the annual summer encampment:

Adjutant's Office Military Academy
West Point, N.Y., July 5, 1841

Orders

No. 35

During the encampment the duties of the 4 classes of cadets will be in addition to the duties prescribed by the army and academic Regulations as follows:

First Class

5 to 7 o'clock a.m. Infantry Drill and broadsword exercise detail to be made by the commandant of cadets and instructor of artillery.

9¼ to 10¼ a.m. Artillery drill and riding, details for this duty to be made by the instructor of artillery.

10¼ to 12½ p.m. Artillery drill, riding, fencing and laboratory exercises, details to be made by the instructor of Art.

2 to 5 p.m. Recitation in artillery, riding and fencing, details to be made by the instructor of Artillery.

5 to 6:20 p.m. Battalion or company drill as the commandant may direct, also dancing.

Second Class

5 to 7 a.m. Infantry Drill.

9¼ to 10¼ a.m. Artillery drill details to be made by the instructor of Artillery.

11¼ to 12¼ p.m. Attendance on squad drill as long as commandant of cadets may direct.

2 to 4¾ p.m. Dancing lessons.

5 to 6:20 p.m. Battalion, company or squad drill.

Third Class

5 to 7 a.m. Infantry Drills.

9¼ to 10¼ a.m. Artillery drills detail to be made by the instructor of Artillery.

11½ to 12½ p.m. Squad drill as long as the commandant of cadets may require.

10¼ to 1 p.m. Dancing lessons after the discontinuance of the squad drills.

5 to 6:20 p.m. Battalion, Company or Squad drills.

Fourth Class

5 to 7 a.m. Infantry Drills.

9¼ to 10¼ a.m. Artillery drill detail to be made by the instructor of Artillery.

11½ to 12½ p.m. Squad drill as long as the commandant of cadets may require.

10¼ to 1 p.m. Dancing lessons after the discontinuance of Squad drill.

5 to 6:20 p.m. Battalion, Company or Squad drills.

By order of Major Delafield
Signed J. Hooker,
Adjt. Mily Acdy

Dancing lessons notwithstanding, it can't have been an easy life, from the start. When the new student reported to the academy, found his room, and presented himself to the upperclassman who would teach him how to be a soldier—that is, how to live at West Point—he became a *plebe* or an *animal*. Next, Morrison recounts,

> the prospective cadet reported to the quartermaster to draw the minimal furniture and equipment he would need for his stay in barracks before taking the entrance examinations. This consisted of a pair of blankets, a chair, an arithmetic text, a slate, a bucket, a tin or coconut dipper, a tin washbasin, a lump of soap, a candlestick, a tallow candle, and a supply of stationery.

Hazing, usually not gentle, and rigid discipline often made matters worse. Joseph James, in a paper I've already mentioned, reports a freshman lament: "During his first month at West Point, George McClellan, who later commanded vast armies, wrote that he felt as 'much alone as if in a boat in the middle of the Atlantic. . . . Not a soul cares for, or thinks of me—not one here would lift a finger to help me.'"

Before the Civil War, many colleges were preoccupied with the development of character. At West Point, Ambrose remarks, "character building reached its apogee":

> The Academy faculty was trying to turn out not just Christian gentlemen but Christian soldiers, so the virtues of duty, loyalty, honor, and courage were emphasized more at West Point than anywhere else. For the cadets, the regulations were stricter and the living conditions worse than for the college students. Jacksonian charges of high living encouraged the Superintendents and their faculties to make the system even harsher. In 1843 Cadet William Dutton took note of their success in a letter to his sister: "All I want of those Editors who say—that 'lily fingered cadets lounge on their velvet lawns—attend their brilliant balls and take pay for it' as I saw in a paper yesterday—is that they may go through but one . . . encampment."

Dutton, class of 1846, resigned due to sickness just after his graduation, became a farmer and manufacturer and a state representative, then showed up in 1862 as a colonel of New York Volunteers, but he died on July 4, 1862, in New York at age 29.

Monotony was also a major factor in cadets' lives. In 1840 Cadet Schureman, whom I've mentioned, wrote to his sister: "At West Point all is monotony. What is said of one day will answer for it almost ten years after."

Monotony. Hazing. Rigid discipline. And more rigid discipline. Cadet George Cushing walked guard all one September Saturday for "defacing public property"—he had been caught, Ambrose says, "with his feet propped on the table in his room." Little wonder, I suppose, that sometimes they slipped away, perhaps to gather convivially and illegally at the off-limits tavern run by Benny Havens, later celebrated in their song. "Few young men could survive four years on the post without some kind of outlet for their energies," Ambrose remarks; "Robert E. Lee was one of a small number who went four years without a single demerit."

But then life wasn't easy for officers in service, either, as Ambrose says in *Duty, Honor, Country*:

> The nation [say, in 1840] had no potential external enemy. The Indians were there, and to be sure they constituted a serious and continuing menace, but hardly one calculated to excite the imagination of a potential Napoleon. The officer might have been able to ignore the low esteem in which the nation held him if there had been compensations within the service, but there were not. The young graduate of West Point found himself on the very edge of civilization with a few resentful privates to command and a few savages to fight. Or, if he was lucky, he could get a post on the East Coast, where he would almost surely be given a quartermaster's duties—for which he had received no training—and would spend his days adding figures, proving to the auditors that he had not lost a single horseshoe and feeling very much like a common clerk. His pay was 25.00 a month; his possibilities practically none. Line officers received their promotions on a regimental basis; a second lieutenant could move up to first lieutenant or a lieutenant colonel to colonel only when a vacancy occurred in his own regiment. There was no compulsory retirement law, and most officers stayed in the army, and thus in theory in command of their outfits, until they

died. Many lieutenants had to wait twenty-five or thirty years for their captains to die before they could be promoted. Excellence, devotion to duty, heroism—all counted for nothing.

No matter. Young Theodore Lincoln Chadbourne went to West Point in 1839. I don't know all that moved him to do so. I guess I never will. In the West Texas Historical Association paper, Susan Miles pictured him and his family:

> Theodore Lincoln Chadbourne, called "Link" by family and friends, was the oldest of a family of nine and obviously the flower of the family. They lived in a fine old home (still standing) in extensive and beautiful grounds. They needed a large home for when they came together—grandparents, uncles, aunts and cousins— they became a congregation presided over by the Honorable Ichabod Rollins Chadbourne, a distinguished citizen, lawyer, Whig, etc., who had helped to effect the separation of Maine from the State of Massachusetts in 1820. He was a handsome personable man of noble proportions—"May the Lord bless you according to your size," his friends would say—and we get the impression that the first-born at West Point in many ways resembled him. In addition to countless professional chores he maintained as a farm a large acreage in Perry nearby.

In 1952, at the time of the centennial of the founding of Fort Chadbourne, the time she had been preparing for in her quest for information about the young lieutenant, Susan Miles had pictured him in a story in the *San Angelo Standard-Times*:

> Little knowledge of young Link's early life is available here. He was a large blond haired boy and, as the eldest child, was conscious of his responsibilities. A hint as to his character is shown by letters to his family written after he had entered the United States Military Academy at West Point at the age of 17.
>
> Even though life was strict in the academy, young Theodore Chadbourne was proud of his ability to avoid demerits "in a place where demerits are given if the hearth brush is found hanging upside down."
>
> An aristocrat by nature he did not readily surrender himself to army life. His letters show an aloofness, and accompanying loneliness which could not fully be filled by his love for music and art.

A large, blond-haired boy, and aloof. I don't know. I can't be sure. I can't know him at West Point in a personal way.

I can't know him at West Point in a personal way. Still, what happened to all also happened to him. What happened to all was his life, too.

A large, blond-haired boy, and aloof. He went to West Point in 1839, when the academy was proving itself, or about to prove itself, in the army way. Already, Ambrose reports, the academy

> was doing a job no one else could do, a job the Jacksonians wanted done more than they wanted anything else. As a congressional committee pointed out, the railroads that connected Boston with the interior, the harbors in Rhode Island and Connecticut, the Susquehanna and Baltimore and the Baltimore and Ohio Railroads, new roads in Michigan and Arkansas, harbor improvements on the Gulf Coast and Mississippi River—all were the products of civil engineers trained at West Point.

The academy had not yet, in the early 1840s, established itself in the army, but it was about to do so. None of the generals of the time was an academy man, but as Ambrose says, Winfield Scott and Zachary Taylor "recognized the abilities of the young West Pointers and used them extensively." A little later, after his campaign against Mexico City, General Scott remarked:

> I give it as my fixed opinion, that but for our graduated cadets, the war between the United States and Mexico might, and probably would, have lasted some four or five years, with, in its first half, more defeats than victories falling to our share; whereas, in less than two campaigns, we conquered a great country and a peace, without the loss of a single battle or skirmish.

Link Chadbourne's class (1843) provides an example of what West Pointers would do:

39 graduated;
36 either died in service or remained in service for at least ten years;
15 became generals in the Union Army;
4 became generals in the Confederate Army;
30 brevet promotions were won during the Mexican War (brevets being awarded rather than medals).

John Preston Johnstone was killed at Contreras. Jacob John Booker died in San Antonio after service in the Mexican War. Theodore Lincoln Chadbourne was killed at Resaca de la

Palma. George Stevens drowned in the Rio Grande in 1846.
Lewis Neill was wounded in Mexico and died in Texas in 1850.
Robert Hazlitt was killed at Monterrey. Edwin Howe died at
Fort Lincoln, Kansas, in 1850. Charles Edward Jarvis died in
California in 1849. Eight lieutenants died young, during or
soon after the war.

Of thirty-nine who graduated in 1843, thirty-two served in
the Mexican War. Perhaps sometimes a few of them gathered.
Perhaps they sang a verse or two of "Benny Havens, Oh!" An
unsigned item in Oliver E. Wood's *West Point Scrap Book* tells
how the song came to be:

> The lamented O'Brien, formerly an Assistant Surgeon in the
> army, was commissioned a Lieutenant in the 8th Infantry. Before
> joining his regiment he stopped at West Point to visit an early
> friend, Major Ripley A. Arnold, then a first-class man, residing in
> "No. 32 Rue de Cockloft" in the old North Barracks. They made
> many excursions to "Benny's." The song was composed by O'Brien
> and others, and set to the tune of "Wearing of the Green." It soon
> became popular, and from that time to this, all those who have
> learned the way to "Benny's" consider it an old stand-by.

Ripley A. Arnold was a first-class man in 1838. The "lamented
O'Brien" might be John Paul Jones O'Brien, class of 1836,
the only O'Brien to graduate before Arnold. Perhaps a few of
them sang

> Come fill your glasses, fellows, and stand up in a row,
> To singing sentimentally, we're going for to go;
> In the army there's sobriety, promotion's very slow,
> So we'll sing our reminiscences of Benny Havens, oh!

Maybe they even got as far as this verse:

> To our comrades who have fallen, one cup before we go;
> They poured their life-blood freely out *pro bono publico*.
> No marble points the stranger to where they rest below,
> They lie neglected far away from Benny Havens, oh!

Perhaps they sang a few verses, but the survivors didn't send
me the testimony I was looking for. Those I most wanted to hear
from sent no word. Some of those he knew and some of those
who knew him survived to write books—histories, memoirs,
letters—or to have books written about them. I had hoped that

some would tell me about Cadet Chadbourne at West Point,
but they are silent, except, perhaps, to note his death at Resaca
de la Palma without elaboration. U. S. Grant was his classmate, and he was at Resaca, though in a different regiment,
but he tells me nothing except that he and Link Chadbourne
and twenty-nine others signed a petition against a merchant,
John DeWitt, in April 1843, shortly before they graduated.
Samuel French was his classmate; he later wrote *Two Wars:
An Autobiography*, but he left me no message. Neither did
Roswell Ripley, another classmate, who would publish a history
of the Mexican War. I look through the roster of classes just
before and just after his and find an honor roll of notables who
might have left me some testimony: in the class of 1840, maybe
William Tecumseh Sherman or Richard Stoddert Ewell; in the
class of 1841, maybe Don Carlos Buell; in the class of 1842,
maybe William Stark Rosecrans or Abner Doubleday or Daniel
Harvey Hill or Lafayette McLaws or Earl Van Dorn or James
Longstreet; in the class of 1843, besides those I've mentioned,
maybe William Buel Franklin or Isaac Quinby; in the class of
1844, maybe Simon Buckner or Winfield Scott Hancock; in the
class of 1845, maybe Edmund Kirby Smith or Bernard Bee.

But there is no word of Cadet Chadbourne in his West Point
days. Still, maybe a few of them sang and got as far as this verse
(in West Point slang, to "fess" is to make a poor recitation):

When you and I, and Benny, and all the others, too,
Are called before the "final board" our course of life to view,
May we never "fess" on any point, but straight be told to go,
And join the army of the Blest at Benny Havens, oh!

Thirteen

Must I Know You?

Dear God, I don't want to have to remember always who they are, even that they are, all those others out there. Sometimes I'd rather just note, just judge, just pass on. Sometimes I'd rather dismiss them, ignore them all, and celebrate myself as the proper judge of the universe. I don't want to have to remember that all those others are real, and to acknowledge that I remember.

I've just come from a party attended by academic colleagues. I didn't care much for them. I don't want to remember that they are real. If that is reality, I don't much want to be in it.

But I want Link Chadbourne to be real. I don't even believe in lieutenants, but I want him to be real.

That doesn't make much sense. If he's to be real, they have to be real—the one who is perpetually purse-mouthed, the one who speaks in academic clichés, the one who comes from elfin haunts, the one who is grand by self-proclamation, the one who gushes without but wants to be tough within, the one who is stricken with deadly earnestness, the one who is terminally cute, the others.

They are real, and I must know that they are real apart from my judgment of them. They are themselves. They are not merely my perceptions of them, though they are that, too. He must be other than my perception of him. All of them are present, real, there. How am I to read them, and not read only myself reading them? How do we learn to go toward the other?

I can't see or think or live outside my own perceptions, but

all those others out there are not just ghosts inhabiting my perceptions, though they are that, too.

Why was I ready, almost from the start, to acknowledge his reality (if I could find him) but not theirs? Because he went out and died? Because he made himself publicly accountable while they haven't? Did he begin to become real to me only because he chanced to fit my need? I first came upon him at the historical marker and learned that he had died young and far from home at a time when I thought I might, in serving myself, lose my own children or be lost to them. Why wouldn't I grieve for Lieutenant Theodore Lincoln Chadbourne?

My children are real, though I didn't always acknowledge that they were except in relation to me. They do not exist only in relation to me. My children are real. I wait for Lieutenant Chadbourne to be real, as he already is. All the others are real. All of them must be freed of my perceptions. Yet I cannot see or think or live outside my own perceptions. Besides, save for sparse records and a double handful of letters, he doesn't exist except in my perceptions. If I characterize him as I have characterized the others, have I re-created them all to suit myself?

Perhaps. Perhaps that's all it will be in the end. Perhaps not. I can still try to learn to go out toward the others, take their testimony first, hear his.

Fourteen

Resaca de la Palma

The *Cullum Register* shows that Theodore Lincoln Chadbourne was assigned to infantry on June 30, 1843; that he was appointed brevet second lieutenant on July 1, 1843; and that on the same day he was assigned to the 2d Infantry Regiment at Fort Niagara, in Youngstown, New York. He would stay there a few days short of two years, but except that he acquired a piano and a horse, which he later regretted leaving, I know nothing of his time there. Mrs. Denton, in a letter cited earlier, remembered the piano and horse from West Point.

Near what turned out to be the end of his assignment there, on March 28, 1845, Mexico broke off diplomatic relations with the United States. With circumstances worsening, Zachary Taylor was ordered to Texas on June 5, 1845. He would gather his army and make his headquarters at Corpus Christi, Texas.

Chadbourne was promoted to second lieutenant, assigned to the 8th Infantry Regiment, and ordered to Texas on September 10, 1845. He arrived there in late October after the long trip—we know from his letters—that took him down through Toledo, Ohio, on to the Mississippi, down to New Orleans, and past his frustration that it might be next spring before he reached his regiment at Corpus Christi. He first appears in the October 1845 monthly return of the 8th Infantry. He was assigned to Company I, commanded by Captain James McNeill. The other officers were First Lieutenant Collinson Gates and Second Lieutenant James Snelling, both West Point-

ers. Snelling won two brevets in the Mexican War and was
wounded at Molino del Rey. He died in 1855 at age 33. Gates was wounded at Resaca de la Palma but also won two brevets in Mexico. He died in 1849 at age 33. I don't know what became of Captain McNeill. What he found there, I'd guess, was a mixed experience: some pleasure, some discomfort, some pain, and some death. Darwin Payne, in "Camp Life in the Army of Occupation: Corpus Christi, July 1845 to March 1845" (*Southwestern Historical Quarterly*, January 1970), says that

> more than half of the United States' entire army congregated there just inside the territory between the Nueces River and the Rio Grande which was claimed by both Mexico and Texas. The soldiers comprised the biggest assembly of United States regulars since the Revolutionary War. Among their numbers were two who would become presidents of the United States, Taylor and a young, love-starved lieutenant named Ulysses S. Grant. Moreover, a host of fledgling officers who later would become famous in the Civil War served at Corpus Christi. Here the troops' numbers swelled from 1,500 to slightly below 4,000 as they prepared for eventual combat in war with Mexico. The soldiers drilled, practiced marksmanship, reveled in the area's unspoiled wonders, enjoyed the more sophisticated American amusements which soon followed them to that Latin-flavored land, and eventually became disillusioned from bad weather and poor health.

When this "army of observation" that was soon to become the Army of Occupation first came to Corpus, Captain W. S. Henry reports in his *Campaign Sketches*, they found it to consist of only about thirty houses, with just two bars. By August 5, however, he could report that at "Mrs. B's" he had enjoyed some "themales." I take it that he meant *tamales*, for he reported, "I know of nothing more palatable." The *New Orleans Picayune* reported on September 8 that this was "one of the healthiest and pleasantest spots in the world." First Lieutenant R. E. Cochran of the 4th Infantry, who would also die at Resaca de la Palma, wrote his parents on September 4 of the fine sea breeze and of his surprise that so few soldiers were sick. In a letter of September 27 he remarks, "I think we are truly fortunate in coming South at the season we did in getting such a delightful situation and with all so healthy."

Hunting trips deep into the territory revealed country,

Samuel French puts it, "as God made it." One party of five, Captain Henry writes, brought back from a three-day hunt 51 geese, 10 deer, 4 bitterns, 2 cranes, 69 snipes, 18 ducks, 4 curlews, 3 turkeys, and 1 panther. In September the *Picayune* was still extolling the weather, and as late as October, Lieutenant George G. Meade was still writing happily about the climate to his wife.

But then the northers and the rain came—not long, I'd guess, after Lieutenant Chadbourne arrived at the Corpus Christi camp.

Captain Henry reports "the most shocking weather imaginable" by late November, and Surgeon John B. Porter records that "the whole Army . . . might be considered a vast hospital. . . . Hundreds were affected who never entered on the sick report." Lieutenant Colonel Ethan Allen Hitchcock, never too happy with the management of the encampment, records for November 28 (but written much later, in *Fifty Years in Camp and Field*):

> Am quite ill again. Have been sick almost ever since I left Louisiana. Although I have obtained temporary relief two or three times, the trouble (diarrhea) has come back upon me and now prevails with increased virulence. If I value either health or life I may feel it a duty to go away from this climate for a time altogether.

Lieutenant Cochran got a "beautiful cold" trying to build a chimney with sticks and mud and spent Christmas Day in his tent shaking with a chill. Earlier, he had enjoyed Texas, but on the day after Christmas he wrote to his parents: "But take all the Deer, Wild Turkey, &C, Send me back to the United States, Halloo! Stop, I forgot Texas belonging to Uncle Sam; and a mighty poor bargain, I think, he made, even getting it for nothing." Thomas R. Irey reports in "Soldiering, Suffering, and Dying in the Mexican War" (*Journal of the West*, April 1972) that of a total of just over 100,000 soldiers eventually involved in the Mexican War, 1,548 were killed in action, but 10,790 died from disease and exposure. Much of this, I judge, is owing to the lack of training and discipline among the rapidly growing volunteer forces. The American soldier, Irey writes,

> especially the volunteer, generally arrived at one of the staging areas, such as Corpus Christi, Matamoras, or Camargo half-

equipped, poorly trained, and improperly clothed. Ignorant of even
the more basic rudiments of military discipline and routine, the volunteers quickly transformed the camps into miasmic sink-holes of filth and squalor.

Death and illness came most often from diarrhea and dysentery, but yellow fever, catarrh, smallpox, and cholera also occurred. When General Taylor and his troops left Corpus Christi in March for the Rio Grande, they left behind somewhere between 800 and 900 sick soldiers.

Other hazards existed, too, not least insects and snakes, but Corpus Christi was rapidly changing. From a population of about a hundred when the soldiers arrived, the town had grown to around two thousand by January 1846. In July 1845, two bars had been operating; by January 1846, an estimated two hundred bars were serving. James Longstreet, another future general, reports in *From Manassas to Appomattox* on the army theater:

> The officers built a theatre, depending upon their own efforts to reimburse them. As there was no one outside the army except two rancheros within a hundred miles, our dramatic company was organized from among the officers, who took both male and female characters. In farce and comedy we did well enough, and soon collected funds to pay for the building and incidental expenses. The house was filled every night. General Worth always encouraging us, General Taylor sometimes, and General Twiggs occasionally, we found ourselves in fund sufficient to send over to New Orleans for costumes, and concluded to try tragedy. The "Moor of Venice" was chosen, Lieutenant Theodoric Porter to be the Moor, and Lieutenant U. S. Grant to be the daughter of Brabantio. But after rehearsal Porter protested that male heroines could not support the character nor give sentiment to the hero, so we sent over to New Orleans and secured Mrs. Hart, who was popular with the garrisons in Florida. Then all went well, and life through the winter was gay.

Since a variety of singing and dancing acts was also presented at the theater, I found myself wondering if Link Chadbourne had been called in as a pianist, but I have not been able to learn one way or another.

Neither the army nor the plans for possible war (or later, the war itself) had universal support among citizens across the country. *Chronicles of the Gringos,* edited by George Winston

Smith and Charles Judah, gives accounts by eyewitnesses and
combatants, together with responses from home. One young
man in Massachusetts wrote to the *Cambridge Chronicle* ex-
plaining his reasons for not volunteering:

> Neither have I the least idea of "joining" you, or in any way as-
> sisting the unjust war waging against Mexico. I have no wish to
> participate in such "glorious" butcheries of woman and children as
> were displayed in the capture of Monterey, &c. Neither have I any
> desire to place myself under the dictation of a petty military tyrant,
> to every caprice of whose will I must yield implicit obedience. No
> sir-ee! As long as I can work, beg, or go to the poor house, I won't
> go to Mexico, to be lodged on the damp ground, half starved, half
> roasted, bitten by mosquitoes and centipedes, stung by scorpions
> and tarantulas—marched, drilled, and flogged, and then stuck up
> to be shot at, for eight dollars a month and putrid rations.

Later in his letter he refers to Resaca de la Palma, where
the battle had already occurred, as "Ransaca de la Plunder."
Within the army, too, there were critics such as Hitchcock
and Daniel Harvey Hill, later a Confederate general. Hill left
Texas in January 1846, upon being promoted, and published a
harsh indictment of "the ignorance and imbecility of the War
Department" that, he contended, had caused so much suffering among the poorly equipped and training troops at Corpus
Christi. His attack was published with the title "The Army in
Texas" in the *Southern Quarterly Review* of April 1846, under
the pseudonym "H. S. Foote, Esq." Probably the commoner
sentiment, however, was that expressed by Walt Whitman, at
the time editor of the *Brooklyn Eagle*: "Let our arms now be
carried with a spirit which shall teach the world that, while we
are not forward for a quarrel, America knows how to crush, as
well as how to expand!"

Zachary Taylor didn't have all that large an army to work
with, to crush *or* to expand. In 1845 the army line consisted
of fourteen regiments—two of dragoons, four of artillery, and
eight of infantry. The authorized strength was 5,300 men, and
they were spread out over about a hundred different posts,
with men stationed, as Longstreet puts it, "along the northern
frontier from Fort Kent in the northeast of Maine to the west
of Lake Superior, and along the western frontier from Fort
Snelling to Fort Leavenworth, and southward to Fort Jessup in

Louisiana." Just before the Battle of Palo Alto, Taylor's army numbered about 3600 men.

As early as October 1845, Taylor recommended a more forward position for his army. In his dispatch to Washington of October 4, he disclaims any intention of interfering in political affairs and reports that "if our government, in settling the question of boundary, makes the line of the Rio Grande an ultimatum, I can not doubt that the settlement will be greatly facilitated and hastened by our taking possession at once of one or two suitable points on or quite near that river." When negotiations with Mexico failed, the president ordered Taylor on to the Rio Grande, and the forces commenced departing Corpus Christi on March 8, 1846. It was to be a twenty-day march, not unimpeded. Longstreet reports their first near encounter with Mexican forces:

> On the 19th the head of the column approached Arroyo Colorado, one hundred and thirty miles from Corpus Christi. The arroyo was about three feet deep, of salt water. Mexican lancers were on the southern side, and gave notice that they had orders to resist our further advance. On the 21st the army was up and deployed along the high banks of the arroyo, the field batteries in position. General Worth was ordered to make the crossing, and rode at the head of the column. We looked with confidence for a fight and the flow of blood down the salt water before we could cross, but the Mexicans had no artillery, and could not expose their cavalry to the fire of our batteries; they made their formal protest, however, that the crossing would be regarded as a declaration of war.

Longstreet was not alone in his confidence and hope. Indeed, some of the regular army officers—Meade, Edmund Kirby Smith, and Philip Barbour, for example—wanted to engage and to defeat the enemy forces before any volunteer troops arrived.

Taylor set up a supply base at Point Isabel, then moved on to the Rio Grande, twenty-six miles away. Theodore Lincoln Chadbourne arrived with his regiment on the Rio Grande opposite Matamoros on March 28, 1846. According to Oliver L. Spaulding's *United States Army in War and Peace*, "Taylor at once commenced the construction of a battery on the river bank for four 18-pounders, and laid out a large bastioned fieldwork behind it. This site was not particularly well chosen, for it was in a bend of the river, and the Mexicans promptly built batteries of their own, crossing fire on it."

On April 30 and May 1, General Mariano Arista crossed the Rio Grande in force below Taylor's position. Taylor apparently soon realized that his supply base at Point Isabel was vulnerable. Longstreet tells what happened next:

> On the 1st of May our tents were struck, wagons parked, assembly sounded, and the troops were under arms at three A.M., marched at four o'clock, and bivouacked within ten miles of Point Isabel. No one was advised of the cause of movements, but all knew that our general understood his business. He had been informed that General Arista, with his movable forces, had marched to Rancho de Longoreno, some leagues below us on the river, intending to cross and cut us off from the base at Point Isabel. Major Jacob Brown was left in charge of the works opposite Matamoras with the Seventh Regiment of Infantry, Captain Sands's company of artillery, and Bragg's field battery.

Taylor's troops arrived back at Point Isabel on May 2 and began preparing the supply base for possible attack. When fortifications at Point Isabel were satisfactory, Taylor started his army back to the Rio Grande on May 7.

The Mexican Army stood in his way on May 8 at Palo Alto, and again the next day, May 9, at Resaca de la Palma.

To tell what happened at Resaca de la Palma on May 9, 1846, I start with General Taylor's report to Washington dated May 17 (House Executive Document No. 209, 29th Congress, 1st Session). Taylor's bastion on the river was named Fort Brown to honor Major Brown, who died of wounds received in the bombardment.

HEADQUARTERS ARMY OF OCCUPATION
Camp near Fort Brown, Texas, May 17, 1846

Sir: In submitting a more minute report of the affair of "Resaca de la Palma," I have the honor to state that, early on the morning of the 9th instant, the enemy, who had encamped near the field of battle of the day previous, was discovered moving by his left flank, evidently in retreat, and perhaps at the same time to gain a new position on the road to Matamoras, and there again resist our advance.

I ordered the supply-train to be strongly packed at its position, and left with it four pieces of artillery—the two 18-pounders which

had done such good service on the previous day, and two 12-pounders, which had not been in the action. The wounded officers and men were, at the same time, sent back to Point Isabel. I then moved forward with the columns to the edge of the chapparal, or forest, which extends to the Rio Grande, a distance of seven miles. The light companies of the first brigade, under Captain C. T. Smith, 2d artillery, and a select detachment of light troops, the whole under the command of Captain McCall, 4th infantry, were thrown forward into the chapparal to feel the enemy, and ascertain his position. About 3 o'clock I received a report from the advance that the enemy was in position on the road, with at least two pieces of artillery. The command was immediately put in motion, and about 4 o'clock I came up with Captain McCall, who reported the enemy in force in our front, occupying a ravine which intersects the road, and is skirted by thickets of dense chapparal. Ridgely's battery, and the advance under Captain McCall, were at once thrown forward on the road, and into the chapparal on either side, while the 5th infantry and one wing of the 4th was thrown into the forest on the left, and the 3d and the other wing of the 4th on the right of the road. These corps were employed as skirmishers, to cover the battery, and engage the Mexican infantry. Captain McCall's command became at once engaged with the enemy, while the light artillery, though in a very exposed position, did great execution. The enemy had at least eight pieces of artillery, and maintained an incessant fire upon our advance.

The action now became general; and although the enemy's infantry gave way before the steady fire and resistless progress of our own, yet his artillery was still in position to check our advance, several pieces occupying the pass across the ravine which he had chosen for his position. Perceiving that no decisive advantage could be gained until this artillery was silenced, I ordered Captain May to charge the batteries, with his squadron of dragoons. This was gallantly and effectually executed. The enemy was driven from his guns, and General La Vega, who remained alone at one of the batteries, was taken prisoner. The squadron, which suffered much in this charge, not being immediately supported by infantry, could not retain possession of the artillery taken, but it was completely silenced. In the mean time the 8th infantry had been ordered up, and had become warmly engaged on the right of the road. This regiment and a part of the 5th were now ordered to charge the batteries, which was handsomely done, and the enemy entirely driven from his artillery and his position on the left of the road.

The light companies of the first brigade, and the 3d and 4th regiments of infantry, had been deployed on the right of the road, when, at various points, they became briskly engaged with the enemy. A small party, under Captain Buchanan and Lieutenants Wood and Hays, 4th infantry, composed chiefly of men of that regiment, drove the enemy from a breastwork which he occupied, and captured a piece of artillery. An attempt to recover this piece was repulsed by Captain Barbour, 3d infantry. The enemy was at last completely driven from his position on the right of the road, and retreated precipitately, leaving baggage of every description. The 4th infantry took possession of a camp where the headquarters of the Mexican general-in-chief were established. All his official correspondence was captured at this place.

The artillery battalion (excepting the flank companies) had been ordered to guard the baggage train, which was packed some distance in the rear. That battalion was now ordered up to pursue the enemy, and, with the 3d infantry, Captain Ker's dragoons, and Captain Duncan's battery, followed him rapidly to the river, taking a number of prisoners. Great numbers of the enemy were drowned, in attempting to cross the river near the town. The corps last mentioned encamped near the river; the remainder of the army on the field of battle.

The strength of our marching force on this day, as exhibited in the annexed field report, was 173 officers and 2,049 men; aggregate, 2,222. The actual number engaged with the enemy did not exceed 1,700. Our loss was three officers killed, thirty-six men killed and seventy-one wounded. Among the officers killed I have to regret the loss of Lieutenant Inge, 2d dragoons, who fell at the head of his platoon, while gallantly charging the enemy's battery; of Lieutenant Cochrane of the 4th, and Lieutenant Chadbourne of the 8th infantry, who likewise met their death in the thickest of the fight. The officers wounded were Lieutenant Colonel Payne, inspector general; Lieutenant Dobbins, 3d infantry, serving with the light infantry advance, slightly; Lieutenant Colonel McIntosh, 5th infantry, severely, twice; Captain Hooe, 5th infantry, severely (right arm since amputated;) Lieutenant Fowler, 5th infantry, slightly; Captain Montgomery, 8th infantry, slightly; Lieutenants Selden, Maclay, Burbank, and Morris, 8th infantry, slightly. A tabular statement of the killed and wounded is annexed herewith.

I have no accurate data from which to estimate the enemy's force on this day. He is known to have been reinforced after the action of the 8th, both by cavalry and infantry, and no doubt to an extent at least equal to his loss on that day. It is probable that 6,000 men were opposed to us, and in a position chosen by themselves, and strongly defended with artillery. The enemy's loss was very great. Nearly 200 of his dead were buried by us on the day succeeding the battle. His loss in killed, wounded, and missing, in the two affairs of the 8th and 9th, is, I think, moderately estimated at 1,000 men.

Our victory has been decisive. A small force has overcome immense odds of the best troops that Mexico can furnish—veteran regiments, perfectly equipped and appointed. Eight pieces of artillery, several colors and standards, a great number of prisoners (including fourteen officers), and a large amount of baggage and public property, have fallen into our hands.

The causes of victory are doubtless to be found in the superior quality of our officers and men. I have already, in former reports, paid a general tribute to the admirable conduct of the troops on both days. It now becomes my duty, and I feel it to be one of great delicacy, to notice individuals. In so extensive a field as that of the 8th, and in the dense cover where most of the action of the 9th was fought, I could not possibly be witness to more than a small portion of the operations of the various corps, and I must therefore depend upon the reports of subordinate commanders, which I respectfully enclose herewith.

Colonel Twiggs, the second in command, was particularly active on both days, in executing my orders and directing the operations of the right wing. Lieutenant Colonel McIntosh, commanding the 5th infantry; Lieutenant Colonel Garland, commanding the 3d brigade; Lieutenant Colonel Belknap, commanding the 1st brigade; Lieutenant Colonel Childs, commanding the artillery batallion; Major Allen, Captains L. N. Morris and Montgomery, commanding respectively the 4th, 3d, and 8th regiments of infantry, were zealous in the performance of their duties; and gave examples to their commands of cool and fearless conduct. Lieutenant Colonel McIntosh repulsed, with his regiment, a charge of lancers, in the action of Palo Alto, and shared with it in the honors and dangers of the following day, being twice severely wounded. Lieutenant Colonel Belknap headed a charge of the 8th infantry, which resulted in driving the enemy from his guns, and leaving us in possession of that part of the field.

Captain Duncan and Lieutenant Ridgely deserve special notice for the gallant and efficient manner in which they manoeuvred and served their batteries. The impression made by Captain Duncan's battery upon the extreme right of the enemy's line at the affair of Palo Alto contributed largely to the result of the day; while the terrible fire kept up by Lieutenant Ridgely, in the affair of the 9th, inflicted heavy losses upon the enemy. The 18-pounder battery, which played a conspicuous part in the action of the 8th, was admirably served by Lieutenant Churchill, 3d artillery, assisted by Lieutenant Wood, topographical engineers. The charge of cavalry against the enemy's batteries, on the 9th, was gallantly led by Captain May, and had complete success. Captain McCall, 4th infantry, rendered distinguished service with the advance corps under his orders. Its loss, in killed and wounded, will show how closely it was engaged. I may take this occasion to say that, in two former instances, Captain McCall has rendered valuable service as a partisan officer. In this connexion, I would mention the services of Captain Walker, of the Texas Rangers, who was in both affairs with his company, and who has performed very meritorious services as a spy and partisan. I must beg leave to refer to the reports of subordinate commanders for the names of many officers, non-commissioned officers, and privates, who were distinguished by good conduct on both days. Instances of individual gallantry and personal conflict with the enemy were not wanting in the affair of the 9th, but cannot find place in a general report. The officers serving on the staffs of the different commanders are particularly mentioned by them.

I derived efficient aid on both days from all the officers of my staff. Captain Bliss, assistant adjutant general, Lieutenant Colonel Payne, inspector general, Lieutenant Eaton, aide-de-camp, Captain Waggaman, commissary of subsistence, Lieutenant Scarritt, engineers, and Lieutenants Blake and Meade, topographical engineers, promptly conveyed my orders to every part of the field. Lieutenant Colonel Payne was wounded in the affair of the 9th; and I have already had occasion to report the melancholy death of Lieutenant Blake, by accident, in the interval between the two engagements. Major Craig and Lieutenant Brereton, of the Ordnance department, were actively engaged in their approximate duties; and Surgeon Craig, medical director, superintended, in person, the arduous service of the field hospitals. I take this occasion to mention, generally, the devotion of duty of the medical staff of the army, who have been untiring in their exertions, both in the field and in the hospitals, to alleviate the sufferings of the wounded of both armies. Captains Crossman and Myers, of the Quartermaster's department, who had charge of the heavy supply train at both engagements, conducted it in a most satisfactory manner, and finally brought it up, without the smallest loss, to its destination.

I enclose an inventory of the Mexican property captured on the field, and also a sketch of the field of "Resaca de la Palma," and of the route from Point Isabel, made by my aide-de-camp, Lieuten-ant Eaton.

One regimental color (battalion of Tampico) and many standards and guidons of cavalry were taken at the affair of the 9th. I would be pleased to receive your instructions as to the disposition to be made of these trophies—whether they shall be sent to Washington, &c.

I am, very respectfully, your obedient servant,
Z. TAYLOR,
Bvt. Brig. Gen. U.S. Army, commanding
The Adjutant General of the Army,
Washington, D.C.

General Taylor's report can be supplemented by Lieutenant Colonel W. G. Belknap's report to Taylor, dated May 15 (I omit Belknap's report on Palo Alto and his closing observations and commendations). Belknap, who had commanded the 8th Infantry, was at Resaca in command of the 1st Brigade, which included the 8th:

On the morning of the 9th, we were instructed to assume the same order, and advance upon the enemy, he having in the night and early in the morning retired. The brigade advanced across the plain, and took position in the chapparal, where we halted for several hours, waiting instructions, and burying in the meantime eleven of the enemy's dead, that were there found terribly mangled. The army having been put in march in the afternoon, the brigade was ordered to halt as a reserve, when within about a mile of the enemy's position. In a few minutes, the firing having commenced in front, I received orders to move up Duncan's battery and one battalion of infantry. The battery and the 8th regiment were immediately put in motion, the latter in double quick time.

On arriving at the scene of action, the 8th regiment charged the enemy on the right of the road, and drove him from his position. At this moment Captain May, of the 2d dragoons, informed me that he had charged and carried one of the enemy's batteries; but, being unsupported, was unable to maintain it. I immediately ordered the 8th infantry to form in the road, when it was led to a charge upon the battery, a part of which had, as reported, been re-taken by the enemy. This movement was executed with the greatest celerity, and the battery secured. The regiment then charged upon the ravine and across the small prairie amidst a sheet of fire from the front and right, drove the supporting column before it, destroying the enemy in vast numbers—they having maintained a most determined and obstinate resistance until finally repulsed and driven from the field. Captain Montgomery, with his regiment, pursued vigorously into the chapparal on the opposite side of the ravine, until, from the rapid flight of the enemy, further pursuit was useless.

The conflict was short—the result shows with what severity.

At the head of the ravine, I met with Captain McCall, 4th infantry, who, in command of the advance, had gallantly brought on the action and poured a most destructive and kept up an incessant fire upon the enemy.

After the commencement of the action, on advancing with the 8th infantry and the battery of artillery, I ordered Lieutenant Colonel Childs to remain with his battalion as a reserve. It is due to Colonel C. to state that he was desirous that his battalion should be selected to advance into the action, instead of the 8th regiment. He soon after received orders from the commanding general to advance. He obeyed, and rapidly pursued the enemy to the Rio Grande, where, having thrown out pickets, he captured one captain and about twelve privates during the enemy's flight.

As soon as the enemy's batteries were carried, and his infantry began to give ground, Captain Duncan was ordered to cross the ravine and take up a new position, that previously occupied rendering it impossible for him to assail the enemy without galling our own troops. This was done, and the enemy vigorously pursued; a few well-directed shots from our batteries driving him from position to position till he reached the river.

Where all have acted nobly, it may seem improper to speak of individuals.

But that isn't enough. I wanted to know what happened and where on the battlefield it happened, specifically where the 8th Infantry Regiment was and what it did, more specifically where Lieutenant Chadbourne was, what he did, and how he died.

Some of that I am, I think, not going to be able to learn.

In preparing the little chronology of the Battle of Resaca de la Palma that follows, I have relied on diverse sources; these are listed in a bibliographical note at the end of the book.

Of the sources I've used, the following authors were near or close contemporaries of Lieutenant Chadbourne at West Point (graduating class in parentheses following name) and at or near the battle: French (1843), Longstreet (1842), Sedgwick (1837), Meade (1835), Stevens (1839), Grant (1843), Ephraim Smith

(1826), Henry (1835), Barbour (1834), Ripley (1843), and Wilcox (1846).

After their defeat by the Americans on May 8 at Palo Alto, the Mexican Army retreated only a short distance, and most expected that the Mexicans would renew the battle. Indeed, George Kendall, whose work I cite a little later, treated Palo Alto and Resaca de la Palma as one battle. At any rate, on May 9, 1846, some six thousand Mexican troops still barred Taylor's path back to his fortification on the Rio Grande.

Some of the Mexican soldiers were visible at daybreak in the thick chaparral and mesquite. "Early the next morning," Longstreet reports, "a few of the Mexican troops could be seen, but when the sun rose to light the field it was found vacant. A careful reconnoissance revealed that the enemy was in retreat, and the dragoons reported them in march towards our comrades at Fort Brown."

The Americans spent the early hours of May 9 looking over the previous day's battleground, hunting for any overlooked wounded, and burying the dead.

General Taylor went back to his supply train to send a report off to Washington. He ordered an entrenchment prepared around the parked wagons and left about 500 men as guards. He had departed Point Isabel with well over 2,000 soldiers and about two hundred supply wagons. After leaving a guard for his supply wagons, he had about 1,700 soldiers to take into battle against more than 5,000 Mexican troops.

When he had done what was possible to secure his supply train, Taylor went forward himself with about 120 infantry to scout the enemy and the terrain.

About four miles from the Rio Grande, he found the Mexican Army well situated across the road that would take him back to his river fortification. They were entrenched and fortified before, within, and behind "the concavity of a horseshoe curve in what had once been a channel of the Rio Grande." This was the Dry Canyon or Dry Channel of the Palms, the battleground of Resaca de la Palma. At times, some have called it Resaca de Guerrero. Most believe that these are two names for the same place. Bancroft says that Resaca de Guerrero is the place where the Americans halted before engaging the Mexicans and that Resaca de la Palma is the place where the battle occurred. All seem to agree that on both sides of the channel the growth of chaparral and mesquite was uncommonly thick. Some disagreement occurs, however, about the nature of the channel itself. The most common account, I judge, is that the dry channel was mostly four to five feet deep and perhaps some two hundred feet wide, the bottom cluttered with brush, stagnant ponds, and stunted palms. Edward Nichols reports that it was about fifty yards wide and about ten feet deep. Justin Smith reckons it several hundred feet wide and three to four feet deep. Charles L. Dufour calls it only about fifty feet wide but eight to ten feet deep. John Frost, in *The Mexican War and Its Warriors*, describes the setting in this way:

> At this place the road crosses a ravine sixty yards wide and nearly breast high, the bottom being wet, forming long and serpentine ponds through the prairie. Along the banks of this dry river, and more particularly on the side then occupied by the Mexicans, the chaparrel grows most densely, and at this time, save where it was broken in by the passage of the road, formed almost a solid wall. The enemy occupied this ravine in double line; one behind and under the front bank, and the other entrenched behind the wall of the chaparral on the top of the rear ridge. A battery was placed in the center of each line on the right and left of the road, and a third battery was on the right of the first line. Six or seven thousand troops were thus strongly fortified in a form resembling a crescent, between the horns of which the army had to pass, while the Mexican batteries were enfilading and cross firing, the narrow road which formed the only unobstructed approach to their position.

In his *Pictorial History*, Frost adds that

> the ridges on each side are covered with dense rows of chaparral, utterly impenetrable to horse, and defying every weapon save the bayonet. . . . In the thicket nearest the Americans, as well as in the ravine below, . . . the enemy lay in double rows; and another line of them extended through the chaparral on the opposite bank. Three batteries were placed so as completely to sweep the road, their fires at the same time crossing each other. Through such a pass, defended by six thousand veteran soldiers, must Taylor's little army of less than two thousand men pass.

In *War with Mexico*, Roswell S. Ripley, Chadbourne's classmate, presents the scene in this way:

Arista had been re-enforced during the morning by near two
thousand infantry and a strong body of cavalry. His infantry occupied the northern crest of Resaca de la Palma, which ravine is crossed by the main road from Point Isabel to Matamoras at a point some four miles from the latter place. The general outline of the ravine is an irregular curve, of which the convexity is given to the south. The road running toward the south crosses the ravine about the center of its length. Three guns on the northern crest defended the point of passage, and two on each side of the road south of the ravine supported the first battery with a flank and cross fire. Along the southern crest was posted a second line of infantry, and the cavalry, which were necessarily unable to act, was in strong masses to the rear. The position and disposition of the Mexican forces were exceedingly strong against an enemy advancing by the road, and the thick growth of chaparral rendered such an advance the one most probable, if not absolutely necessary. But the same cause rendered a complete view of the operations impracticable, and made any action at the point one of detail on both sides, with the advantage, however, of a knowledge of locality on the part of the Mexicans not possessed by their enemy.

The batteries on the rear, or south side, of the ravine, according to Jenkins and others, were "supported by veteran infantry regiments, and the Tampico battalion, a brave and well-appointed corps." The 8th Infantry would be instrumental in ending the battle by going through the ravine, up and over the entrenchments on the south side, and against these troops.

Packed lines of Mexican skirmishers, then, held the thickets on the near, or north, bank, with others in the ravine and heavy support waiting on the south bank. Artillery, some of it entrenched, was positioned to sweep the road, and any attack would be exposed to flanking fire. The thorny undergrowth was so thick that Taylor's use of artillery was limited except on the road, and the brush made coordinated movements by infantry impossible for any unit larger than a platoon or, at most, a company. The Mexican Army clearly had the advantage of position. Justin Smith, however, points out a disadvantage for the Mexicans—the condition of the troops:

Many, and probably most of them, had not eaten for more than twenty-four hours. The sufferings they had witnessed and the neglect of their fallen comrades from the day before at Palo Alto had worked upon their feelings. The dreadful effectiveness of the American artillery had been profoundly discouraging; many of their officers had proved unworthy of confidence.

This was the setting for the Battle of Resaca de la Palma. The action that ensued there, from all accounts, was an extraordinary demonstration on both sides of courageous and sustained intensity and personal valor in all ranks.

Taylor moved to engage the enemy at about 2:00 P.M., sending Captain McCall forward with an advance party from the 4th Infantry, together with some artillery troops and Captain Walker's Texas Rangers.

The Mexican guns opened on them with grapeshot and canister. Ringgold's battery of six-pounders, now under the command of Lieutenant Ridgeley, went into action on the road, moving to within about three hundred yards of the Mexican guns before preparing to fire.

At about the same time, American infantry deployed in successive lines of skirmishers on both sides of the road, moving through the thick growth as the Mexicans advanced to meet them. The 5th Infantry and about half of the 4th Infantry were on the left, and the 3d Infantry and the other half of the 4th on the right. The 8th Infantry was being held in reserve. The early action is described in an especially valuable book, T. B. Thorpe's *Our Army on the Rio Grande* (1846):

> The moment that Ridgely received orders to advance, he moved forward and cautiously along the road, endeavouring, with the assistance of Capt. Walker, to obtain the exact position of the enemy's batteries, which they finally discovered in the road, in advance of their own columns. At this instant the batteries opened fire, and Lieut. Ridgely and men charged them at full speed, and with loud cheers, in which they were joined by the Fifth Regiment, who were in the van of the infantry. The Fifth, now deployed as skirmishers, pushed on at full speed nearly three-fourths of a mile before Ridgely opened, and with a speed nearly equal to that of the flying artillery. A portion of the Fourth soon came up, and joined with the Fifth on the left, and the Third Regiment and the remainder of the Fourth came towards the ravine on the enemy's right . . . thus almost simultaneously, our musketry opened with our artillery, and the action of Resaca de la Palma commenced.

The battle, as Alfred H. Bill puts it, quickly degenerated "into
numerous isolated combats in which a squad or two, a platoon,
or, rarely, a whole company fought it out with bayonet and
clubbed musket against groups of Mexicans who contended
for every glade and thicket with stubborn courage." Ripley remarks that "each captain and subaltern led his command as an
independent body." One of Grant's letters describes the fight
as "a pel mel affair every body for himself. The chapparel is
so dense that you may be within five feet of a person and not
know it." Justin Smith says that

> companies found it impossible to remain intact. A field officer was
> no more than a captain, and a captain no more than a subaltern.
> All got into the work promptly, and all did their best when there.
> As fast as they could, singly or in little squads, they pushed on,
> cheering and shouting. Often it required one's utmost exertions to
> squeeze through or hack through the dense and thorny chaparral
> under pelting showers of bullets. Now there was shooting, and now
> the cold steel struck fire.

H. H. Bancroft says it was "dare-devil work."

Meanwhile, a party of Mexican lancers caught Ridgeley's
battery as he was moving the guns forward, some say to within
a hundred yards of the enemy. He had only one gun unlim-
bered. Sergeant Kearnes rammed home a load of canister on
top of a shell and fired quickly, taking out all but four of the
charging lancers. Ridgeley charged them single-handed and
was able to drive them off. Once in action, however, his six light
pieces could only hold their own, and the Mexican artillery
continued to sweep the road and the thickets on either side.
The American infantry could make only slow progress—when
they made any at all. "The best troops of Mexico," Thorpe
writes, "were now disputing for the honor of their arms . . .
the struggle was terrible. The enemy disputed every inch of
ground, never yielding except when overcome by force."

Zachary Taylor, sitting on his horse, Old Whitey, under
threat of artillery fire, reckoned that he and his staff should
move up so that the rounds might go over them.

Thorpe reports, but not all agree, that it was at about
this time—now nearing 4:00 P.M.—that the 8th Infantry was

brought up from its position in reserve. Some report that it was not only brought up but went into the mixed action. What seems likeliest, from Taylor's later report and from other sources, is that the 8th was brought up into readiness along the right of the road but not yet put into action.

At about the same time, Taylor, reckoning that his troops could make no further progress under the galling Mexican artillery fire, ordered Captain May to charge the Mexican batteries with his dragoons. What followed was much publicized at the time and was credited by some contemporaries, and by some more recent historians, with ending the battle.

It didn't.

Captain May apparently took his orders to charge from General Taylor and rode off, only to return a little later to tell Taylor that the Mexican artillery had changed position. Taylor, it is commonly reported, told May, "Charge, captain *nolens volens!*" As May and his dragoons rode into action, they passed Ridgeley and his batteries. Ridgeley called out to May either "Hold on, Charley," or "Wait, Charley, till I draw their fire." May then led his squadron of dragoons at a gallop down the road and into the batteries.

But despite Ridgeley's help, some of the Mexican artillery had remained ready and loaded, and they now opened fire on the dragoons. It was then, I believe, that First Lieutenant Zebulon Montgomery Pike Inge of the dragoons was killed.

The dragoons went on and may have taken some guns twice but could not hold them either time. They overran the guns on the near, or north, side of the ravine, went down into the ravine, and made it almost up the far side. They took heavy losses, and May could gather only a few, perhaps six, for their formation was broken and some horses were uncontrollable by now. With the few he could gather, May wheeled and charged back the way he had come. The Mexican gunners had taken cover in the nearby brush. On his way back through, May may have captured General de la Vega, who had not taken cover, but the reports differ about who actually first took the general prisoner. At any rate, the dragoons hit the guns twice and dismanned them, but could not hold them, and the Mexican gunners returned and commenced firing again.

Some disagreement occurs about what happened next, but I
think the common judgment is plain: the 8th Infantry entered.

Some do not mention the 8th Infantry's part in the battle. Among Chadbourne's contemporaries, for example, Samuel French was chiefly preoccupied with the role of the unit he was with at the time, Ridgeley's artillery, and after May's charge says only that "at that moment our infantry opened on them, and all was over in our immediate front." U. S. Grant doesn't mention the 8th. In his letter dated May 9, 1846, George Meade doesn't mention any specific units. Longstreet doesn't mention specific units. E. Kirby Smith doesn't mention the 8th but does attribute most of the action around and after May's charge to his own 5th Infantry. Among later writers, Ladd, for example, reports that the 8th was moved up early and that the 5th Infantry went in after May's charge to take the guns. Weems does not mention the 8th but credits the 5th Infantry. *The Mexican War*, by the editors of Time-Life Books, with text by David Nevin, omits the 8th Infantry and gives primary credit to the 5th.

General Taylor's report, however, which I have already quoted, says that May's squadron,

> which suffered much in this charge, not being immediately sup-
> ported by infantry, could not retain possession of the artillery taken,
> but it was completely silenced. In the mean time the 8th Infan-
> try had been ordered up, and had become warmly engaged on the
> right of the road. This regiment and a part of the 5th were now
> ordered to charge the batteries, which was handsomely done, and
> the enemy entirely driven from his artillery and his position on the
> left of the road.

Colonel Belknap's report gives essentially the same testimony: the 8th Infantry had already come up from reserve, was engaged, and then took the charge into the Mexican artillery and to the far, or south, bank of the ravine.

I should remember that this was a riotous, confused scene, that even eyewitnesses can only see some parts of any complex action, and then not well. If, in war, credit is owed, it is in this instance owed to all, including the 8th Infantry.

As I am able to piece it out, the chronology of events following May's charge features the 8th Infantry.

When May and his dragoons were unable to hold the Mexican guns, which had, despite Taylor's report, apparently resumed firing, Taylor turned to Belknap, evidently in some exasperation and concern, and said, "Take those guns and, by God, keep them."

The 8th charged down the road. Many reports agree that the regiment went "with fiendish yells" or "yelling like fiends." With them were some troops from the 3d Infantry under Captain Barbour who had been in the fighting on the right of the road. Also with them were Duncan's battery and troops from the 5th Infantry under Captain Martin Scott, who had been on the left of the road. Oliver Spaulding says simply that "the guns could not be held until the 8th Infantry came up and took them."

They went through the ravine and into the brutal fighting up against the opposite bank, then up and over it, taking the guns and breaking the Mexican strength on the road and to the left of the road, or the Mexican right. Central to the opposition met by the 8th and the others was a crack veteran battalion, the Tampico Guards. The two sides met in sword-to-sword, bayonet-to-bayonet, hand-to-hand fighting.

General Arista had stayed in his tent almost up to this time. When he came out and saw the circumstances, he put himself at the head of General Anastasio Torrejon's lancers and led them to the attack. He was too late. His charge was beaten back. When the Mexican center broke, the Mexican strength on the right broke. The whole army gave way and ran toward the Rio Grande. Most of the American units gave chase. Some overran General Arista's camp, taking his personal belongings. I believe that it was in the last fighting near Arista's camp that Lieutenant Cochran fell. The Americans chased the retreating Mexicans past their camp, where packs were still in order on the ground, fires were still burning, and beef was still hung up ready for cooking, but there was no real pursuit all the way to the river. By about 5:30 it was over.

Why was I interested in the 8th Infantry? Because I was still looking for Lieutenant Chadbourne, looking to know what he did, where he was, how he died.

Among Chadbourne's contemporaries, Ripley puts the 8th

in the thick of things and reports that when May could not hold the Mexican guns, General Taylor

> had sent orders to Lieutenant-colonel Belknap to advance one regiment from the guard of the train, and at this time he led the eighth infantry into action. Moving down the road in column at a charging pace, the eighth, joined by a portion of the fifth, which had beat through to the ravine on the left of the road, crossed the ravine, secured the guns, and, pushing into the chapparal, after a severe struggle drove the enemy from the vicinity.

Ripley's account, in other words, shows that the 8th was still back in reserve when told to charge.

Variations are inevitable. Thorpe, in *Our Army on the Rio Grande* (1846) reports that May, returning from his charge, came to Colonel Belknap of the 8th with the message that unsupported, he was

> unable to maintain it [the enemy's main battery]; Colonel Belknap immediately ordered the regiment to form in the road, when he led it on in person. While advancing, he was joined by a part of the Fifth Infantry under Capt. M. Scott. For an instant, the fire of the Mexicans checked the advance, when Col. Belknap sprang forward, and seizing one of their standards, waved on his troops, who were now, with the entire Fifth Regiment, engaged in hand-to-hand conflict with the celebrated Tampico veterans. In the charge, Col. Belknap had the staff of his standard shot away, and on the same instant his horse, coming among a pile of dead and wounded artillerists, made a sudden movement aside, and threw his rider. The Eighth took up the cry that their commander was killed, and dealt their blows all the heavier, when he appeared at the head of his column; the battery having been carried. The Eighth, then under the immediate command of Capt. W. R. Montgomery, and the Fifth, under Lieut. Col. McIntosh, charged up the ravine amidst a sheet of fire from the enemy's right and front. They drove their supporting columns before them, repulsing charges of cavalry and infantry of immense superiority of force, and although killing vast numbers, with difficulty driving the enemy from the field. . . . Lieut. Chadbourne of the Eighth, after distinguishing himself for his bravery, in one of these skirmishes fell mortally wounded, at the head of his command.

A little later, Thorpe also reports on the death of Lieutenant Cochran. Cochran, some other young officers, and diverse soldiers had come upon Arista's camp when they encountered a Mexican officer. Thorpe does not claim that it was Arista himself. They fired on the officer:

> Undauntedly he moved, held his ground, and received a volley of musketry, and most singularly he remained upon his horse, and rode off. A moment only elapsed, when he returned with a squadron of lancers, charging like a whirlwind; our soldiers delivered their fire steadily, bringing one or two horsemen to the ground, and then fell back into the chapparal. Lieut. Cochran remained in the open space, and received the whole charge; he nobly defended himself with his sword, but was crushed down, falling dead with seven lance wounds in his breast.

Frost's *Pictorial History* (1848) reports that

> May charged a gun with but five men. The 8th infantry, under Colonel Belknap, advanced to his assistance, their leader bearing a standard in front through a storm of musketry. As his soldiers closed with the Tampico troops, the conflict became more terrible than it had been before, and the wild shouts and imprecations of infuriated thousands wrestling for victory, with every passion aroused, united with the clashing of swords and bayonets, and formed a scene alike exciting and terrible. Colonel Belknap was thrown from his horse, and the command devolved on Captain Montgomery. Some of the troops fought breast deep in water, while others cut down the chapparal with their swords, in order to afford their comrades an opportunity to enter.

Frost adds in *The Mexican War and Its Warriors* (1850) that the 8th and the 5th "were engaged in a hand-to-hand conflict with the far-famed Tampico veterans, who had been in twenty battles and were never defeated."

Captain W. S. Henry, in his *Campaign Sketches* (1847), remarks only that the 8th was "conspicuous" in the attack that finally silenced the artillery and broke the Mexican infantry.

According to some contemporary reports, it seems likely that fewer than twenty of the Tampico Guards survived the battle.

Among later writers, Bancroft, for example, pretty well follows General Taylor's report in situating the 8th infantry. Theophilus Rodenbaugh and William Haskin add that in addition to the Tampico Guards another famous veteran regiment, the Lapadores, also faced the 8th.

Joseph Sides indicates that the 8th came up early, "at double
time, in columns of companies, proceeding under destructive
showers of grape." This *before* their charge into the ravine.
Nichols also pretty well follows Taylor's account; unlike
Sides, he supposes that the 8th was still in reserve when it was
ordered to charge.

On June 5, 1846, the *New Orleans Daily Picayune* carried
a letter from a writer in Matamoros who signs the letter only
"Justice." For what seems an equitable distribution of credit, I
quote the entire letter:

Gentlemen: In looking over your paper of the 17th, containing various accounts of the victories of the 8th and 9th, my attention was
especially called to a letter written from "Camp Victory," giving
you, apparently, a detailed description of the two battles. As you
have sent the latter forth to the world, with your endorsement of
your belief of its truth, permit me to make a few remarks upon it,
and beg their insertion in your paper. Your letter-writer, an "officer of the rank in the army," has claimed the credit of the battle
of the 9th for the gallant Capt. May and the 5th infantry. No one
doubts Capt. May's gallantry and the important service rendered
by his brilliant charge; but when all the honor of that charge is
claimed by your correspondent for the 5th infantry, it is "piling it
on a shade rather too mountainously," and it is charity to presume
that he wrote under the disadvantages of hurry and the confusion
of such a scene. No one would detract from the merits of that gallant regiment, nor would the writer of this deprive it of one iota of
its justly earned praise, for its gallantry and efficiency in the battle
of the 9th, and for its full share of the credit of that never to be forgotten charge. But I go for doing justice *to all,* and not leaving the
public under the impression that the other regiments composing
our gallant little army were mere "lookers on in Vienna." Let our
motto be, "render unto Caesar the things that are Caesar's." It is
well known that owing to the confusion attending the flight, from
the separation and intermingling of the different regiments, aris-
ing from their impetuosity and the thickness and impassablity of
the chaparral, officers and men of different regiments were mixed
together fighting side by side; and that the force constituting the
charging column, which supported the gallant May and secured
the fruits of his intrepidity, was made up from men and officers of
the 3d, 4th, 5th, and 8th regiments of infantry—the 8th having beyond a doubt the largest proportion. There can hardly be a question

that the gallant 8th, *as a regiment*, was in the thickest of the fight. Their return of killed and wounded speaks volumes. The 5th also suffered severely and were in positions where the balls fell thick and fast, as if *bushels of hickory nuts* had been shot at them; but the writer must recollect that by their side were parts of the 3d and 4th infantry, Capt. McCall's advanced guard and Capt. C. F. Smith's battalion of light companies. I do not mention Duncan and Ridgeley's batteries, for they are just *patched with glory*. There are also more claimants to the taking of those "five pieces of artillery" than the 5th. The battle was not won by the gallantry of that regiment *alone*, but by the impetuosity and daring of the stout hearts of *all*. It was the misfortune of the artillery battalion to be left in charge of the train; no one doubts but they would have given a good account of themselves. There is glory enough for the whole, and it seems, to say the least, unfortunate and in excessively bad taste that any writer should attempt to claim the honor of the victory for any *one* regiment.

Why was I interested in the 8th Infantry Regiment? Because I was still looking for Lieutenant Chadbourne, looking to know what he did, where he was, how he died.

I'm still not certain exactly how the 8th was situated, except at the first and the last. At the first, the regiment was held in reserve, guarding the supply train. At the last, the regiment was in the middle of terrible fighting. In between? I'm not certain. Either they were still in reserve when ordered to attack, or they had moved up "under destructive showers of grape" to become engaged along the right side of the road, only to be ordered by Belknap to form in the road and charge. Wherever they were, they charged down the road, into the ravine, and up and over the artillery and guns on the far side.

Perhaps it doesn't matter too much where they were when they began their charge: the distance through the enemy forces, from wherever they started, was at most only about two thousand yards.

And where was Lieutenant Chadbourne? What did he do? How did he die? Where was he when he died? I'll have to come back to that a little later.

Two days after the battle, General Taylor congratulated his troops on the "brilliant impetuosity" with which they had carried the enemy position. About 1,700 American soldiers had gone against an estimated 6,000 Mexican soldiers. Early on,

Mexican losses were estimated at about 1,200 for the two days of Palo Alto and Resaca de la Palma. Spaulding suggests 160 Resaca de killed in the Mexican Army, 228 wounded, and another 159 la Palma missing, but reckons that the numbers were probably much higher. The *Handbook of Texas*, however, accepts the same number of Mexican losses: 547 killed, wounded, or missing. American losses were 39 killed and (probably) 89 wounded. The Americans had captured eight guns, two hundred stands of arms, two hundred pack mules, 150,000 rounds of ammunition, General Arista's personal luggage and papers, and the standard of the Tampico Guards.

I was wrong in much of what I said when I first wrote about Chadbourne and the fort. I was far off the mark when at the outset I said it might have taken two months for his parents to learn about his death. It surely didn't.

Word of the Battle of Resaca de la Palma reached Washington, D.C., on May 23, 1846, just *two weeks* after the battle, and the first notice was in the *New York Herald* on May 24, with these headings:

EXTRAORDINARY EXPRESS FROM NEW ORLEANS
and
LIGHTNING LINE, TO NEW YORK

TELEGRAPHIC DISPATCH NO. 1

HIGHLY IMPORTANT
FROM THE RIO GRANDE

GLORIOUS NEWS

TWO TREMENDOUS BATTLES

TWELVE HUNDRED MEXICANS
REPORTED TO BE KILLED

THE MEXICAN ARMY
TWICE ROUTED

THE MEXICAN GENERAL, VEGA, CAPTURED

THE AMERICAN ARMY
TRIUMPHANT

THE DEFEAT OF THE MEXICANS
AT THE POINT OF BAYONET

This first story (with all the headings above) does not, I believe, convey any information that I have not already given. Neither does the second, on May 25. On the third day, Tuesday, May 26, more details begin to appear, including the names of some of the dead and wounded: "General Taylor lost sixty men, among them Lieut. Inges of the dragoons, Lieut. Cochran, of the 4th Infantry, Lieut. Chadburn, of the 8th Infantry." The next day's paper, that for May 27, spells his name right and gives his home state. The *Herald* for May 28 features a letter from a young dragoon officer who was in May's charge. It includes this:

> We lost some few officers and men. Among the officers was poor Lieutenant Inge—he had just joined, and was killed in the charge on the enemy's batteries; I charged by his side, and was unhorsed, and doubtless thus escaped. I am too grateful, first for the opportunity of being in the fight, and then to escape unhurt.

Earlier, I listed some of my sources but reserved some of the most useful. One of the latter I've since cited, Thorpe's *Our Army on the Rio Grande* (1846). N. C. Brooks, *A Complete History of the Mexican War* (1849), already cited, has been particularly helpful. To these, I'll now add the *Picayune* and the *Herald* and George W. Kendall's *War Between the United States and Mexico* (1851), to which I'll return later.

The dead of Resaca de la Palma were buried near where they fell. "On the 10th," Captain Henry writes, ". . . we were actively employed burying the dead. Lieutenants Inge, Chadbourne, and Cochrane were buried with funeral honors; the unsodded grave by the road side, with its rude paling, marks the spot where sleep those who died gallantly in battle." An eyewitness reported to Frost, as he records it in his *Pictorial History*, that

> Resaca de la Palma is covered with the graves of our fallen countrymen, who fell, many of them, fighting hand to hand with the enemy. Their antagonists are buried around them by hundreds. I was shown one grave, near the spot where the brave Cochrane is interred, in which eight Mexicans are said to have been placed; and there are many more, each containing a score or two of the slaughtered foe. The grave of poor Inge was pointed out to me. It was with deep feelings of sadness that I recalled to mind the many virtues of this gallant and noble-minded officer.

Thomas Wilhelm's *History of the Eighth U.S. Infantry*, carries this notice with some minor error in graduation:

> Lieutenant Chadbourne, one of the most gallant soldiers, has, in his heroic death, won fame for himself, and left a proud record for his Regiment. He was born in Maine, and appointed from the Military Academy, Brevet-Second Lieutenant 8th Infantry, September 10th, 1845, and was killed in action at the head of his command, at the age of twenty-three years. He was buried at Camp near Brownsville (to which place the Regiment marched immediately after the battle) with appropriate military honors. Captain J. V. Bomford performed the funeral ceremonies.

His remains were later taken to Eastport, and later still a monument was put in place: "His last acts are part of his country's history. The memory of his frank and ingenuous disposition, of his love of excellence and devotion to duty, and of his high and generous aims is deeply surgraved on the hearts of the friends and associates of his youth by whom this monument has been raised."

And surely enough, eventually I found again the note I started with on the first page, in Colonel Belknap's report to General Taylor: "In the battle of the 9th, the 8th regiment lost, in Lieutenant Chadbourne, a promising young officer, who fell in the manful discharge of duty."

When Theodore Lincoln Chadbourne died at Resaca de la Palma, the United States had not yet officially declared itself at war. He was not less dead for that.

Fifteen

Death and Silence

But none of that was enough. I wanted to know where he was, and what he did, and how he died, and where he was when he died.

Perhaps I wanted it to be as I thought it was in boyish, and therefore doubly deluded, imagination, as when I first read *Beau Geste* and came to think that's how it is or ought to be: the death of a comrade will forever be significant, will tell on you down through the years. I wanted witnesses to tell me what I thought I wanted to know. His death would stay, and they would tell. In James Warner Bellah's novel *The Apache*, the central character, First Lieutenant Flintridge Cohill, on leave from cavalry duty in the West, has gone back to West Point:

> That night in Winfield Scott's old bedroom he stood for a long time staring out the window across the sleeping post, and there was a consciousness of the concept of progression that had never come upon him before. There in cadet barracks the young fledglings slept, and there and there and there were the last metallic likenesses of those who had gone before and paid in one way or another the full price of commitment to a personal gage of honor. He stood among them now himself, with the course part run and well run and the final stretch long years ahead of him still. Clay Sitterding and D'Arcy Topliff, who had marched here with him as boys, lay dead far out on the north reaches of Crazy Man Creek. And there were others of lesser friendship scattered all along his last ten brutal years. . . . He blew out the candle and stood alone with the ghosts of

the place crowded close about him. Lundy's Lane and Plattsburg.
Bladensburg and the Florida swamps. Chapultepec, Contreras, and Vera Cruz. Bull Run to Appomattox Courthouse. Beechers Island, the Little Big Horn. And the battle honors seemed somehow then to run on without horizon far beyond him into names and times he could not know . . .

I wanted them to tell me, those who might have been witnesses, but they didn't. I didn't expect much from General Taylor, and I didn't get much: "Among the officers killed I have to regret the loss of Lieutenant Inge, 2d dragoons, who fell at the head of his platoon, while gallantly charging the enemy's battery; of Lieutenant Cochrane of the 4th, and Lieutenant Chadbourne of the 8th infantry, who likewise met their death in the thickest of the fight."

But I expected to learn about him from his classmates and fellow junior officers. I should have known better. Most or all couldn't tell: some weren't there; the battlefield was an unholy confusion; if they were there, they may have been separated; if they were together, they may not have seen him; if they saw him, they may have seen wrong and then misremembered.

Some of them were too far removed from him in their time at West Point for that connection to count. Ephraim Kirby Smith, class of 1826, says, "I saw no man falter and the object of each seemed to be to find the largest crowd of Mexicans. It is a glorious fact for the army that there were no volunteers with us." But he only notes in passing that Inge, Cochran, and Chadbourne were lost. Philip Norbourne Barbour, class of 1834, reports only that "Lieuts. Nege [I take it that he didn't know Inge], Cochrane, and Chadbourne fell gallantly in this action." William Seaton Henry, class of 1835, mentions the deaths of the three lieutenants, and I have already cited his notice of their burial. George Gordon Meade, class of 1835, does not mention Chadbourne in his letters. John Sedgwick, class of 1837, had not yet arrived on the Rio Grande, and it's a pity, for he writes good letters. Isaac I. Stevens, class of 1839, does not mention Chadbourne; he is mostly busy refuting the judgments of Roswell Ripley. James Longstreet, class of 1842, only mentions the deaths. Cadmus Marcellus Wilcox, class of 1846, only mentions the deaths. Perhaps each did all he could or thought appropriate.

But the reports of Chadbourne's three classmates are a different matter. Samuel G. French, U. S. Grant, and Roswell S. Ripley were all of the class of 1843. I expected more from them and was sometimes frustrated, sometimes angry when they did not give more.

Sometimes I swore at them. They were there. They might have told me.

French's *Two Wars: An Autobiography* was not published until 1901. That alone may account for the silence, I suppose. He remembers some things well, but others, I guess, are gone. Early in the book, he remembers—and reproduces—a boycott signed by thirty-one first classmen on April 15, 1843: "We, the undersigned, do hereby agree that we will purchase nothing from John DeWitt after this date, except what we have already ordered, or whatever is absolutely necessary, the reason being supposed manifest to every one." DeWitt was the sutler at West Point; apparently he had caused some of the young men to be put on report. French's name is signed, and Grant's, and Ripley's. T. L. Chadbourne also signed the boycott notice. French, long since a general by 1901, reproduces a letter from General Rufus Ingalls to General Isaac Quinby, which Quinby sent on to French. Ingalls and Quinby also signed the notice. Receipt of Ingall's letter through Quinby sets off French's recollections:

> My dear, good Rufus! How I recall the many happy days we have passed together! My love for you was like unto Jonathan's for David, and you have gone and left me, gone to your long home. Yet I can see you now. I can see you at the card table having "fun" even though the "time to be 4 A.M." There always was mirth when Ingalls was present. He was the prince of good fellows; ever cheerful, never selfish, full of quaint humor, and was wont to "set the table in a roar."

But French and Ingalls, I assume, shared a long friendship. The letter is dated September 16, 1889; Ingalls died in 1893, before French's book was written. Chadbourne, however, died in 1846. French, who was with Ridgeley's artillery at Resaca de la Palma, does not mention him.

The boycott notice, I should mention, is also reproduced in the papers of U. S. Grant. Grant does not otherwise mention

Chadbourne, though in two early letters—one to Julia Dent
on May 11 and one to John W. Lowe on June 26—he does tell about the battle.

Ripley's is the most damnable account. *The War with Mexico* was published in 1849, not such a long time after May 9, 1846. He gives due credit to the 8th Infantry:

> When the action [May's charge and Ridgeley's artillery support] had fairly commenced, General Taylor had sent orders to Lieutenant colonel Belknap to advance one regiment from the guard of the train, and at the time he led the eighth infantry into action. Moving down the road in a column at a charging pace, the eighth, joined by a portion of the fifth, which had beat through to the ravine on the left of the road, crossed the ravine, secured the guns, and, pushing into the chapparral, after a severe struggle drove the enemy from the vicinity.

But of Chadbourne himself, he says only this: "Of the Americans, thirty-nine were slain, including three subalterns of merit: Inge of the Dragoons, Cochrane of the fourth, and Chadbourne of the eighth infantry."

Chadbourne was a "subaltern of merit." How strange, from a classmate.

But perhaps not so strange. Of those who might have known and seen him, some waited for years to write and perhaps forgot. Of those who wrote early, some didn't see him, some saw but didn't remember, and some, perhaps, remembered but didn't think to say it in a public document. A "subaltern of merit."

(When what was not the end—most things don't have an end—but a stopping place for this piece of work was near, I began to dream. I don't find in this any special intensity. It's just my way of fretting, and maybe hoping. I had been looking especially for firsthand accounts of Lieutenant Chadbourne, maybe in his West Point years, maybe in camp at Corpus Christi or on down at the resaca. Maybe someone would tell me just how he died and just where he was. But it began to look as if I were running out of possible sources. They weren't telling me what I hoped to know. Still unexamined sources might tell me something directly about his West Point life, but I was at or near the end of possibilities for learning about his last months

and days. I began to dream. I dreamed of finding the source
that would tell about him. Mostly, I dreamed of finding un-
published manuscripts written by participants in the Battle of
Resaca de la Palma. On two consecutive nights, I dreamed that
I had found a book-length unpublished manuscript written by
James Longstreet. Then I quit dreaming about it. Just as well—
Longstreet was a poor candidate.)

A "subaltern of merit." My God! Why the detached report?
Why the silence?

Even if they knew to speak and had been inclined to speak,
I'd guess that diverse versions of protocol kept them mostly
silent. To many of them, of course, a detached report ("three
subalterns of merit") was the only kind of report appropriate. Time passed for some before they wrote; they had become
generals, and generals think important thoughts. Time passed.
Look at a college or high school yearbook, friend, and try to
detail what happened even to those who were close friends.
Mostly, you can't. Try to detail what happened even to that
person in the yearbook picture who bears your name. Mostly,
you can't. Then, too, they were inheritors and creators of male
protocol: a man's got to do what a man's got to do, and he
shouldn't expect a memorial notice for it. And there's that other
protocol: second lieutenants die. That's what they do, and they
mostly don't get much notice. If they don't die, after a while
they get promoted.

I learned a little more about how he died and where he was
from apparent strangers. Sometimes they do better, but they
don't always resolve conflicts.

The truth is, I still don't know for sure what he did, where
he was, how he died, or where he was when he died. I think I
know, but I'm not sure.

He was with the 8th Infantry Regiment.

The regiment, at least at first, was held in reserve to guard
the supply train.

After that, I'm uncertain.

Two common but divergent accounts of the regiment's first
movements exist. According to one account, as I've already said
(chapter 14), the regiment stayed in reserve until ordered by
General Taylor, through Colonel Belknap to Captain Montgomery, to charge after May had been unable to hold the guns,

whereupon they went down the road at a "charging pace," over
the ravine's north bank, into the ravine, up and over the guns on the south bank, and into the heavy hand-to-hand fighting there. According to the other account, the regiment had already come up from reserve and was on the road and engaged to the right of the road when General Taylor ordered them to "take those guns and, by God, keep them."

Whether they charged into the ravine from their reserve position or from a forward position, it seems likely that they charged under heavy fire from Mexican guns using grapeshot.

In either case, Lieutenant Chadbourne was with them, though not all the way.

I think they came up from their reserve position, which wasn't all that far anyway, proceeding, as Sides puts it, "under destructive showers of grape."

I suppose it's possible that Lieutenant Chadbourne died in the artillery fire as the 8th Infantry was moving up. The *New Orleans Picayune* for June 13, 1846, digests "a minute account of the actions of the 8th and 9th May." It was written by a second lieutenant of the 8th Infantry for his father in New York and originally published in the *Spirit of the Times*. The author may have been Alfred St. Amand Crozet, the only second lieutenant in the 8th Infantry who had been appointed to West Point from New York. At any rate, the *Picayune* quotes part of the account:

Having now given the general outline of the battle, I will now give my particular experience. We advanced, as I said before, the road, not dreaming of seeing an enemy, when we heard the firing in our front. Presently Capt. Duncan came galloping down the road, and I heard him say it was a small party covering the retreat of the others. The next order I heard was, for Capt. Duncan's battery to advance, and advance they did, and with terrible execution. The next was, "*make way for the dragoons*," and we opened to the right and left, and they dashed through to charge the cannon, we cheering them as they passed. The next order was "*8th Infantry, forward*," and away we went. On the first battlefield, I picked up the musket of one of the wounded men of my company, thinking it a better weapon than my sword. As I was rushing I found both too much trouble to carry, so I threw the sword into a wagon by the road-side, and kept on with the musket. A turn in the road brought us exposed to the fire of grape from the enemy, which came thick and fast, but I noticed with great pleasure that most of it went over our heads, and to our left in the bushes. We lost some men by them, and poor Chadbourne I think was killed by them. *"I'm gone,"* was all he said.

This may be the firsthand account of his death that I was looking for. I'm not sure. Other accounts seem as persuasive, or more persuasive. If this is where he died, it probably means that the "destructive showers of grape" came not as they were moving up but as they were charging to take the guns that May could not hold.

I believe the 8th Infantry had moved farther, was already into the ravine and fighting against the entrenched Tampico Guards and others on the south bank when Lieutenant Chadbourne fell. George Kendall of the *Picayune* was on the Rio Grande shortly after the battle, visited the battleground, and talked with witnesses. He reports that after May's charge, when the infantry went in,

> the hard tug was yet to come; for the opposite banks were lined with the enemy, the thick brush in the rear was alive with skirmishers, and they clung to their ground with a pertinacity which showed they were determined not to yield. Their continuous fire still ravaged every approach, and their shrill cries, contrasting strangely with the more lusty shouts of the Anglo-Saxons, were heard coming up from every part of the dense cover in which they were contending. Yet the assailants still pressed them vigorously, the men using their bayonets and the officers laying about with their swords as they advanced. In a regular pell-mell, for all order had previously been lost, the Americans crossed the ravine, in many places waist deep in mud and water. Officers found themselves leading strange men—the men were following officers unknown to them—yet one desire, to close with the Mexicans, still animated all alike, and up the opposite bank in the face of a sharper shower than ever, and into the cover still full of men, they plunged with a spirit that never flagged. Several younger officers were killed; the veteran McIntosh was shot down and bayoneted; Payne, the acting inspector-general, was also badly wounded in the midst of the melee, while the men fell thick and fast. So firmly did the Mexicans hold to their ground, that the bayonet only could loosen them; and this was freely used. As they finally retired they continued the fight; but Belknap having brought the entire 8th Infantry into the struggle, and uniting his

efforts with those of Garland and other officers, the men were at length launched upon such a shock that every part of the line was carried.

T. B. Thorpe, author of *Our Army on the Rio Grande* (1846), like Kendall, was soon on the scene, collecting materials for newspapers, and he tells much the same story in a passage I have already quoted:

> Col. Belknap immediately ordered the regiment to form in the road, when he led it on in person. While advancing, he was joined by a part of the Fifth Infantry under Capt. M. Scott. For an instant, the fire of the Mexicans checked the advance, when Col. Belknap sprang forward, and seizing one of their standards, waved on his troops, who were now, with the entire Fifth Regiment, engaged in hand-to-hand conflict with the celebrated Tampico veterans. . . . The Eighth, then under the immediate command of Capt. W. R. Montgomery, and the Fifth, under Lieut. Col. McIntosh, charged up the ravine amidst a sheet of fire from the enemy's right and front. They drove their supporting columns before them, repulsing charges of cavalry and infantry of immense superiority of force, and although killing vast numbers, with difficulty driving the enemy from the field. . . . Lieut. Chadbourne of the Eighth, after distinguishing himself for his bravery, in one of these skirmishes fell mortally wounded, at the head of his command.

Later in his book, in the "Anecdotes and Incidents" section that follows his account of the battles, Thorpe adds a chilling note: "Lieut. Chadbourne was killed, when in the act of taking possession of a battery, by two lancers; a brother officer avenged his death, by almost instantly killing both of the Mexicans with his sword."

Thorpe took some pains to be thorough. His account includes lithographs of the graves of Chadbourne, Inge, and Cochran, and an account of their burial:

> Early on the morning following the victory, Gen. Taylor sent over to Matamoros for Mexican surgeons, to attend their wounded left on the field, and also for men to assist in burying their own dead. It was an occasion of sadness to our troops, for the day was occupied in burying their brave countrymen, who had fallen on the battle field. These honored dead were laid in their last resting-places, near the spot on which they fell. . . . Lieut. Inge and his fellow dragoons rest side by side, but a little removed from the place where they fell: as

the traveller crosses the ravine, he can, by turning a few paces from the road, rest a moment by these graves.

Lieutenant Chadbourne fell in the deadliest struggle of the Eighth. The sod that drank his life-blood, now rests over him. Nearer the river, the road turns, leaving an open space upon the right, in which is a grave slightly distinguished from those about it; Lieut. Cochrane there sleeps his last sleep.

And Thorpe includes eulogies for the dead:

LIEUT. THEODORE LINCOLN CHADBOURNE
EIGHTH REGIMENT OF INFANTRY

Lieut. Chadbourne, who was killed on the Resaca de la Palma, in the deadly charge of the Eighth regiment, was a native of Eastport, Maine. He was of most excellent military descent, being great-grandson of Maj. Gen. Lincoln of the Revolutionary Army. He met his death long before he had arrived at the prime of manhood, being but twenty-three years of age; yet he had already shown traits of character that marked him among the most promising of the young officers of our little army. He is represented to have been a model of manly beauty, possessing a mind that harmonised with his symmetry of person. He was singularly happy in all his associations with his brother officers. He was the idol of the domestic circle, and the pride of his parents. His death carried sorrow into the happiest of family circles, and destroyed well-cherished hopes that built bright scenes of glory for the warm-hearted and patriotic soldier.

Lieut. Chadbourne was a graduate of West Point, and had been two years in the army. Upon the receipt of the news of his death, at Fort Niagara, the United States officers there stationed, held a meeting, expressive of their sorrow at his death, and of their admiration of him as a man and a soldier.

I wish that I could know all of it for sure, or any of it.

I learned enough to know that I accepted too quickly the hope of relative and friend. In a letter to Susan Miles in November 1951, Mrs. Frederick Denton, daughter of Tom Chadbourne, the lieutenant's young brother, wrote that "in the uniform of that day there was, I think, a white belt around the waist and a white strap extending from the belt diagonally over the left shoulder. On that strap was embroidered some sort of ornament, like a daisy, which was placed directly over the heart of the wearer." And, Susan Miles continued, "through the center of that flower-like ornament, she stated, passed the bullet

that killed Lieutenant Chadbourne." I expect that they both
wanted to believe that he found quick and neat death.

I doubt it.

If his tunic is not at Fort Concho, there may be good reason.
He may have been buried in it. It may have been too torn to
show. His death may have been sudden, but I'd guess it wasn't
neat. Grapeshot comes not as a single bullet but as many, and
the thrusts of lancers make ragged tears.

I wish they had told me everything so that I could be sure.
They didn't. They were silent. But someone out there named a
fort for him.

Sixteen

Fort Chadbourne

How in hell can I be mad at those others for getting things wrong or for leaving things out or for not telling what I thought I wanted to know? I'm not doing too well myself.

For a while, I lost track of what Colonel Belknap said about Lieutenant Chadbourne. I was wrong about how much time it took for word of the battle and of his death to get back to the East. I never did see his tunic; it was never there. I expect I was wrong about the neat bullet hole, maybe hoping, like others before me, that it was a quick, neat death. I may be wrong about where he was and how he died. I don't think so, but I may be wrong. (A crudely sketched map in the United States Military Academy archives, probably made on the battlefield, shows the 8th Infantry in the lead along the road and to the right, facing the Mexican guns in the road, the guns on the farther crest of the ravine, and the entrenchments of the Mexican troops, including the Tampico Guards. I think that's where he was, going up the far side, when the lancers came.)

And, at least at first, I was wrong about the fort. That first time, when I stopped casually to read the historical marker about halfway down the road from Abilene to San Angelo, I thought I had the fort located. The marker is on a low bluff above the highway.

Fort Chadbourne:
Established by the United States Army, October 28, 1852, as a protection to frontier settlers against Indians. Named in honor of

Lieutenant T. L. Chadbourne killed at Resaca de la Palma, May 9, 1846. Occupied by Federal Troops, 1852–1861, 1865–1867. An important station on the Butterfield Overland Stage Route, 1858–1861.

The account in Robert Frazier's *Forts of the West* seemed to verify that, though the two don't agree in every particular:

CHADBOURNE. Established October 28, 1852. Located on the east side of Oak Creek about three miles above its junction with the Colorado River and about four miles northeast of the present town of Fort Chadbourne. Established to protect the emigrant route from Fort Smith, Arkansas, to Santa Fe. Established by Captain John Beardsley, 8th U.S. Infantry. Named for Second Lieutenant Theodore L. Chadbourne, 8th U.S. Infantry, killed on May 9, 1846, in the Battle of Resaca de la Palma. Surrendered to the Confederacy on March 23, 1861, by order of Brigadier David E. Twiggs. Reoccupied by the United States on May 25, 1867, and partly rebuilt. Abandoned as a regular post on December 18, 1867, because of the failure of the water supply, but irregularly used as a picket-post and garrisoned from Fort Concho for about a year thereafter.

That seemed all right, but then I remembered that I had seen no sign of any creek, not even a dry creek bed, when I first pulled over to read the historical marker.

Then I found out what anyone who paid attention would have already known: the site of the fort is not anywhere close by the marker. It is elsewhere, on private property where tourists are not entirely welcome, at least not just any time.

And the ruins are fairly extensive. The fort has not disappeared, as I had thought.

Ray Miller's *Texas Forts* puts the fort off U.S. 277, ten miles north of Bronte (pronounced BRONT) in Coke County, and reports that the post was first called the Camp on Oak Creek, then Camp Chadbourne, then Fort Chadbourne. Miller locates the fort on the east side of Oak Creek about thirteen miles above its junction with the Colorado River. He adds that there were three stone buildings (two barracks and the hospital), the rest of log and canvas. Accompanying pictures show the surviving ruins. In his *Eyes of Texas Travel Guide* for the area, Miller also mentions the town of Fort Chadbourne, as Frazier did. I didn't at first know about it. Joe Gibson's *Forts and Treasure Trails of West Texas* gives much the same information. Herbert M. Hart's *Old Forts of the Southwest* relates the story of the man who survived fourteen arrows; he was fortified, Hart says, by liquor bought at the Dutchman's hut across the creek. "Ruins of the saloon," Hart says, "can still be seen across Oak Creek from the post." I haven't seen the ruins of the saloon. That doesn't mean they aren't there. Charles M. Robinson's *Frontier Forts of Texas* says the ruins are on the Chadbourne Ranch. He also reports, as Hart does, that Cynthia Ann Parker was seen among visiting Indians at the fort before her recapture by whites.

Well, anyway, it's in Coke County. After it ceased being a fort, maybe it was the Odom Ranch. Then maybe it was the Wylie Ranch. Now it's the Chadbourne Ranch.

Jessie Newton Yarbrough, in *A History of Coke County*, is specific in her directions:

> The ruins of old Fort Chadbourne occupy a beautifully situated spot in the northeast corner of Coke County, on a flat, wooded promontory on the east bank of Oak Creek, thirty miles above its juncture with the Colorado River.
>
> The route to the site of the old fort may be reached by traveling along Highway Seventy, north from San Angelo or south from Sweetwater to a point nine miles north of Bronte and six miles south of Blackwell where Highway 158, "The Butterfield Trail," intersects Highway 70. Turning eastward at that point, one travels approximately three miles to a bridge across Oak Creek. As he approaches the bridge, he notes a large marker in a shady spot beneath the oaks near the roadside.

The plaque on the marker, Yarbrough says, commemorates the Southern Overland Mail Line and recognizes Fort Chadbourne one mile to the southeast. Soon after the bridge, Yarbrough says, there is a road leading to the right, or south, to a gate and a cattle guard, and onto the ranch. Near the entrance, another monument marks the site of Fort Chadbourne.

Actually, Yarbrough's specificity doesn't help me all that much. For one thing, on my enlarged map of Coke County, Highway 158 now goes *through* Bronte, not nine miles north. A second problem: if you go three miles east, as Yarbrough says, you're just about out of Coke County, with no bridge in sight. A third problem lies with my map: it has Fort Chadbourne marked on it in three different places. I couldn't at first account for this, unless one is the fort, one is the town, and the last is the cemetery, which turns out to be the case.

Maybe it was no matter. What originally counted with me was not Fort Chadbourne itself, though I'm interested in forts. What mattered was that someone thought to name a fort for Lieutenant Chadbourne.

Someone, indeed, was trying to name a fort for him sooner than we all thought.

The fort was probably where I think it was, a couple of miles from the first marker I saw on Highway 277. I've marked it on the map. Somehow or another, forts wind up being where we think they are. But I didn't at first know about the other two places that are called Fort Chadbourne on the enlarged county map.

I had to go out there and see for myself. When I did, on Saturday, March 17, 1990, I started from the Day's Inn in San Angelo. I drove first to the marker; that was 49.2 miles from the Day's Inn. I had already arranged to meet Bob Huckabee of the Chadbourne Ranch. I drove there from the marker; that was 1.4 miles. He showed me around a bit, then left me alone to look; and I did, for a long while. Then I drove back to the historical marker, looked at it again, and went on to where I thought the town of Fort Chadbourne was; that was 4.3 miles from the marker. If I was right, the town may be on what is now a dirt road that goes roughly west from Highway 277 just about where the road from Sweetwater joins it.

But first I had to learn about *Camp* Chadbourne. Indeed there was a Camp Chadbourne, but it wasn't out on the other side of Abilene, where the fort was. It was elsewhere. At first, though, I didn't know what I was seeing. In a way, Fort or Camp Chadbourne was farther away than any of us thought, but at first I didn't know what I was seeing.

Fort Chadbourne was established on October 28, 1852, but Camp Chadbourne existed, for a while, three years earlier.

As I was just beginning to try to learn about the place, I ordered the microfilm version of the Fort Chadbourne post returns—the monthly report for the fort—from the National Archives. When I got it, the first entry was peculiar. It said "Camp Chadbourne, 1849, no returns." I mostly ignored that. I guess I thought it was some kind of bureaucratic glitch—everyone knew that Fort Chadbourne was established in 1852.

A little later, I wrote to the Historical Reference Branch of the United States Army Military History Institute, at Carlisle Barracks, Pennsylvania. In reply, I received some bibliographical references and two photocopied file notes. The first was a brief identification of Fort Chadbourne, established on October 28, 1852, and located where it's supposed to be, out beyond Abilene. The second was this:

CHADBOURNE, CAMP   TEXAS

A United States camp—situated in Gillespie County near Fredericksburg and named in honor of Lieut. Theodore L. Chadbourne, 8th U.S. Infantry, who was killed at the battle of Resaca, May 9, 1846.

It was subsequently designated Fort Chadbourne. It was occupied by Companies D, F, I and K, 8th U.S. Infantry in 1849.

Once again, I didn't pay too much attention. Another administrative blooper, perhaps. But then, in Wilhelm's *History of the Eighth U.S. Infantry*, I found the same information in repeated references to Camp Chadbourne, in Gillespie County, occupied in 1849 by 8th Infantry troops. Something was wrong. *That* camp wasn't eventually designated *Fort Chadbourne*. Fort Chadbourne is out beyond Abilene, not down near Fredericksburg. Fort McIntosh, Fort Croghan, Fort Gates, Fort Duncan, Fort Graham, Fort Inge, and Fort Worth were established in

1849 (and Fort Martin Scott maybe at the tail end of 1848), but
not Fort Chadbourne.

But there was a Camp Chadbourne in 1849, and for some
period of time. House Executive Document 93 (35th Congress,
2d Session) contains a report from the secretary of war on ex-
penditures for barracks and quarters in rent, construction, and
repair. No rent expense shows for *Fort* Chadbourne until the
fiscal year ending June 30, 1854. But the report shows construction and repair expense—all of $1.65—for *Camp* Chadbourne
in the fiscal year June 30, 1849.

Eventually I came to believe what the evidence had been telling me all along: there was a Camp Chadbourne in 1849, but
it was never designated Fort Chadbourne. The outline index in
the National Archives shows that Fort Martin Scott was established on December 5, 1848. It was not, however, called that at
first. Post returns from Fort Martin Scott show that for about a
year—from December 1848 to sometime in December 1849—
it was simply called "The Camp Near Fredericksburg." Troops
of the 8th Infantry had arrived there by May 1849. I guess,
then, it must have been during those months of 1849 that some
were unofficially calling it "Camp Chadbourne." Some of the
officers who had been at Resaca de la Palma were there; among
them was John Beardsley, who would later establish Fort Chadbourne, but not for another three years. Cornelius C. Cox kept
a diary of his trip from Texas to California in 1849. For May 11
he records this:

> Arrived at Fredericksburg the evening of the 11th inst—passing
> through the Mormon town four miles below—the Town is situated
> on the North bank of the Perdenales, and has a population of about
> two hundred—there is a Saw and grist mill in the place, and the
> inhabitants appear to be industrious and enterprising—There is at
> this time about two hundred U.S. troops stationed midway between
> the Mormon settlement and Fredericksburg.

Mabelle Eppard Martin, editor of Cox's diary (see *Southwestern Historical Quarterly* 29, 1926), identifies this post as

> Camp Chadbourne, later called Fort Martin Scott. See unsigned
> letter from Camp Chadbourn, April 30, 1849, in *Western Texian*
> (San Antonio), May 3, 1849, and Bartlett's *Narrative*, I, 59. This

last outpost on the frontier was at this time under the command of Colonel Montgomery, who seems to have been very successful in preventing friction between the Indians and the emigrants.

Colonel Montgomery had been at Resaca de la Palma as second in command to Colonel Belknap of the 8th Infantry.

Why does it matter? Because *he* mattered, young Theodore Lincoln Chadbourne. Someone was remembering him; not just in 1852 but also in 1849, as later in San Angelo in 1952. Someone else was trying to find him.

A new line of forts, including Fort Martin Scott, had been built in late 1848 and during 1849, but a scant three years later, more were needed, farther out. In 1851, Fort Belknap, Fort Mason, and Fort Phantom Hill were established. In 1852, Fort Clark, Fort Ewell, Fort Terrett, Fort McKavell, and Fort Chadbourne were added.

Fort Chadbourne was officially established on October 25, 1852, by Special Order 46 from the 8th Military Department:

Head Quarters, 8th Department Camp near Camp Johnstone October 25, 1852

Special Order
No. 46

1. By direction of the General Commanding the Department, the right wing of the 8th Inft will be moved from its present position to a point on Oak creek where it issues from the post oak tract, near the crossing of the creek by Colonel Johnstone's trail of last year and pointed out, by Captain Lee of the 8th Infantry, by the Commanding General on the 21st instant. Two companies will be sent over immediately and the remainder will be dispatched as soon as the necessary transportation can be obtained. The new post will be called "Fort Chadbourne" until the pleasure of the President of the United States be known on the subject. If upon more deliberate and accurate observation of the immediate neighborhood a more preferable location can be discovered, the Commanding Officer is at liberty to select and move the post to such point.

And so it was done by units of the 8th Infantry under the command of Captain John Beardsley. He finished at West Point in 1841, thirty-sixth in his class of fifty-two, two years ahead of young Chadbourne. He had been a first lieutenant, 8th Infan-

try, at Resaca de la Palma. He was severely wounded in the
storming of the enemy's works at Molino del Rey on September 8, 1847, and was breveted captain that day "for gallant and
meritorious conduct." He was born in New York. Sometimes I
have wondered if it was he who wrote accounts of the battle at
the resaca, accounts published without his name in *The Spirit
of the Times* or maybe in the *New York Courier and Inquiries*
or the *New York Gazette and Times.* I expect that I will never
know for sure.

Perhaps, however, I could come to know much about Fort
Chadbourne were I to push toward it. Senate Executive Document 96 (34th Congress, 1st Session), for example, "Statistical
Report on the Sickness and Mortality in the Army of the U.S.,
Compiled from Records of the Surgeon General's Office," tells
much but not all: tells the mean temperatures at the fort for
1852, the monthly rain, and the general weather conditions—
246 days fair, 119 cloudy, 62 with rain, 5 with snow. Jessie
Newton Yarbrough's *History of Coke County* tells about the
lease of the property on which the fort stood and about the
fort's supply and mail sources. Grace Bitner, in "Early History
of the Concho County and Tom Green County" (*West Texas
Historical Association Year Book,* October 1933), provides information on the military units stationed there and on certain
individuals, especially those who went on to greater fame in
the Civil War. Averam B. Bender's *March of Empire* tells of
Robert Neighbors's visit near the fort in the spring of 1853 with
a band of Southern Comanches to discuss their settlement on
land of their own, though action on such a settlement was to be
slow. J. W. Williams, in "Military Roads of the 1850's in Central West Texas" (*WTHA Year Book,* October 1942), reporting
on the establishment of the fort "completely away from beaten
trails," tells of the army roads made to give this fort the outlets it needed. W. G. Freeman's "Report on the Eighth Military
Department" of 1853, edited by M. L. Crimmins (*Southwestern Historical Quarterly,* April 1949), situates the fort better
than most and identifies many of the officers who served there.
Arrie Barrett's "Western Frontier Forts of Texas" (*WTHA Year
Book,* June 1931) recalls the great hailstorm and the great
grasshopper migration of 1854.

Fort Chadbourne was not the fort imagination devises, with a full regiment together with supporting troops, all ready to man the ramparts against the circling Indians—always there in the thousands, no matter how many are killed on-screen. Sometimes, indeed, it was woefully undermanned. During the spring of 1854, for example, when the 2d Dragoons were stationed there, an average of only twenty men, commanded by the post surgeon, were available for duty.

The monthly post returns tell that story best and detail the troops available at Fort Chadbourne throughout its existence.

In "Experiences of an Army Surgeon at Fort Chadbourne" (*WTHA Year Book*, October 1939), M. L. Crimmins tells the story of Dr. Ebenezer Swift, who served at the fort from 1852 to 1856. Albert Sidney Johnston was there on his tour as paymaster in 1855. Robert E. Lee was there in June 1856, gathering the troops he would take on his expedition to the Upper Brazos and past the Double Mountains. Edmund Kirby Smith, then a captain, was there to join Lee's expedition and wondering where to establish a "ranchero." By 1860 he thought he should build his place, just in case Abraham Lincoln were elected. Charles M. Robinson, in his *Frontier Forts of Texas*, tells the story of Major Seth Eastman's choreographed reprisal against the Comanches for the death of two army mail carriers. Colonel J. K. F. Mansfield's "Report of the Inspection of the Department of Texas in 1856" provides details of the situation of the fort and of assignments. Mansfield also provides a map of the fort, as does Herbert M. Hart in *Old Forts of the Southwest*. Hybernia Grace, in "The First Trip West on the Butterfield Stage" (*WTHA Year Book*, June 1932), recounts W. L. Ornsby's trip west, which included a stop at the fort in 1858. Both Rupert Richardson and Joe Gibson tell the story of the famous horse race.

All of them tell about Fort Chadbourne, tell about the people who were there. All of them tell the stories that I wanted to hear, but not all of the stories.

None of them, however, tells me anything about Lieutenant Theodore Lincoln Chadbourne.

I have little means left of learning about him except through the few surviving letters. They came by strange routes: down out of Maine, down from West Point and Fort Niagara, down from along the Mississippi, up from Corpus Christi and the Rio Grande, never to Fort Chadbourne, but down along the old Chadbourne Road to Chadbourne Street in San Angelo, and at last to Susan Miles.

Seventeen

Hunting Lieutenant Chadbourne

Katharine Waring told me how, years before, Susan Miles, then active in the County Historical Association, had become interested in the young lieutenant and had set out to learn what she could about him. She told me that the association still had Susan Miles's correspondence with libraries, archival collections, and surviving members of the Chadbourne family. On our second visit, she asked if I would like to see the files. By this time, I was a little eager and said yes. She brought out two boxes, each about the size that would hold a ream of paper. Near the top of the first was a copy of a paper about Lieutenant Chadbourne that Susan Miles had published in the *West Texas Historical Association Year Book*. At the bottom of the second box was a packet of papers separated from the rest. Among them were letters that Lieutenant Chadbourne had written. The original letters.

Ms. Waring allowed me to photocopy the letters. I brought the copies home, but I didn't read them. I wanted to save them. I didn't want the thing to be finished before it was begun. If, when I read the letters, I learned that I had been wrong here and there, I would correct myself. If the letters turned out to be trivial, they mattered because they existed, and the life mattered because it was. History is not out there; it's in here, where

I am. I wanted to save the letters for last because I wanted to believe that he was in them, that he was there.

Almost from the start, of course, I also knew that I might never find him. But I have been looking.

I hadn't expected letters. I had expected only silence, or perhaps the testimony of others. But even when I had copies of the letters, I didn't read them. I saved them for later. I wanted to believe he was there, or perhaps I only wanted to believe that I could find whatever it was I wanted to find.

After a while, I came to the letters. The collection, separated from the rest of the papers in the two boxes that Ms. Waring showed me, contains thirty-three items. Twenty of them are letters written by Theodore Lincoln Chadbourne. Three are letters written to him—two by his uncle, Thomas Lincoln, and one by his brother George. Four are printed or official documents. Six are letters written by various hands to Ichabod Chadbourne, the lieutenant's father. The originals were in the files of the Tom Green County Historical Association, lately removed to the Angelo State University Library. They survive, naturally enough, in various degrees of clarity. I have worked from photocopies, which are no clearer. The earliest letter was written by young Link Chadbourne when he was still sixteen; he writes to the secretary of war on July 19, 1839, accepting appointment as a cadet at West Point. I believe he is in the letters. I want him to be there.

But the sample is small. Only twenty of his letters came this far. He was a boy when they commence, a man when they end; there is, then, no particular reason to expect stylistic consistency. I cannot know the daily details of his schooling or how much that might have determined his way of writing. Most of the letters—perhaps all but one—were written in several sittings; I judge that they were not conceived as continuous, unified compositions. Many of them are in a hurried scrawl. I gather that he did not think of himself as a writer, consciously composing; oftener than not he is answering queries, asking for news, responding to news, telling his news.

These conditions notwithstanding, I think it is possible to learn about him from the letters, supposing that style does reveal character after all.

I read in him, for example, a steady strain of good humor. He writes to his father on August 28, 1839, still in his first month at West Point:

> I begin to like the place better, as I get used to it. Everything is done fast here, we have to eat fast, sleep fast (if we don't, we don't get enough of either), dress quick, move quick, and think quick. I suppose Mother and Uncle Tom think this will do me no harm, much as I had to alter my habits in these things. I have kept clear of all demerit so far, and I don't care how long it continues to be so.

On December 22, 1839, he writes to his brother George and tells about guard duty: "We have had scarcely any cold weather this fall yet—and I don't care how little there is this winter. The time we feel the cold most is when on Post. We have to go on once a week now and stand about an hour and a half at a time, it is plaguy dull music cold evenings." Writing to George again on July 24, 1840, while on his first summer encampment, he mentions guard duty again—and food:

> This kind of duty is the most tiresome and disgusting that I ever saw, everything is done so strictly and so much by rule. You can't turn your head nor move your body or blow your nose. In addition to this our fare is a little the worst you ever saw. I have always heard that every one has his peck of dirt to eat, but each cadet has at least ten bushels. I don't believe you can tell a much worse story.

A little later in the same letter, he asks George if he has been hunting recently and adds, "We can't do that here, in fact, I don't think of anything we *can* do." In a letter to his aunt Mary at the beginning of his third year, September 12, 1841, he invites her to come visit for a special treat:

> This morning I began my first tour of duty as sergt and commandant of the guards. If you don't come this fall you will not have the pleasure of seeing the guard marched on in style by your loving nephew, for in the spring they have commissioned officers to command the guard, and I have only one platoon to see to. Just now I hear the band playing on the plain. It therefore becometh necessary for me to go out and hear it straightway.

A little later in the same letter, he is back with some remarks about the food:

This is about all I have to say except that the ham smelt so badly to day at dinner that we were obliged to order it off the table: how splendidly the cadets do live! Ham is a new article of food here. It was given to us at the time the fellows began to get sick last encampment, and as medicine is known by its bad taste, what a nice thing our ham must be for sick people.

The good humor persists throughout the letters, even when he is being admonitory, as he often is with George. In a letter to his brother on February 13, 1842, he fusses at the beginning:

O you rascal! you lazy devil! you—you—what the deuce have you been about all this time? What's the use in having you for a brother? I won't own you any longer. Go to thunder! Your letter *did* get here after keeping me in expectancy a month of Sundays. I had quite made up my mind that Miss Wheeler had enticed you off to Texas—The letter was not half filled as usual. What is the reason you don't keep writing a little at a time, no matter how long it takes, until your paper is used up. A fellow might as well be "hung for an old sheep as a lamb," therefore, never pay postage on a half filled letter—Hard at work, you say: no matter, if you can write half a letter you can a whole one: now reform these little errors there's a good fellow.

A few lines along he stops to tell George about a recent innovation at West Point—a riding master has been brought in:

I have taken one lesson in riding, didn't get far enough to start my horse. I hope to next time though: we have to ride a devil of a long time without stirrups, a perfect humbug ain't it? There are five commands before you get into the saddle and that's another humbug; but we do things in military style here.

And then, still in the same letter, he's back to chiding George for the scarcity of news:

What are you doing? Why don't you say more about every day affairs. I am as ignorant as the man in the moon of your concerns and the manner in which you spend your time: every little thing that happens would interest me no matter how trifling: the information that your white hound pup had p——d on the floor was excessively interesting.

He writes to his mother from Fort Niagara on November 5, 1843:

Quite an incident happened a day or two ago—The Corpl of the Guard, an old war soldier who would shoot his brother if ordered to: saw one of the men who had been out without leave on a spree trying to climb the wall, so as to get in unobserved by the sentinels: he ordered him to stand where he was and told a private of the guard to fire upon him if he moved while the corp went round outside to take him—The man sprang for the woods and a bullet after him, but he escaped it. D——n the old fool said the man the next day, he had better be careful, he might have hit me—I suspect however there was no danger for the soldier probably thought he obeyed orders by *firing, hitting* is another affair.

On November 2, 1845, just after arriving at Corpus Christi, he writes to his father:

There is no probability of my seeing any fighting here. The only benefit to be derived is that of seeing so large a force (for our army) of all branches of the service concentrated in one spot. We have brigade drills and are to have the whole army maneuvring together shortly. I was out all day yesterday with the men clearing off the bushes for that very purpose. When we do take to farming we go strong handed I can tell you.

His good humor is there, I believe, in the letters.

(And yet, for a while last summer, I came to disbelieve in my own enterprise, though it's all I have in the way of hunting Lieutenant Chadbourne. We spent a Sunday walking in Williamsburg, Virginia. As we walked and looked at the buildings and exhibits, though I didn't realize at first what was happening, my mood began to shift, so much so that by noon I was tending toward the surly and unmanageable—my wife will give testimony if it's needed. I began to realize that I was disappointed, disconcerted, even angry because much of what I saw in the exhibits wasn't the real thing. The motives of the Williamsburg staff are unquestionable, and their efforts are thorough, efficient, and devoted, but where the real things were not available, they have made facsimiles for display. I wanted to see the real things. Then I came to be more disappointed, more disconcerted, and found myself angrier still: Is that what *I'm* doing? I wondered; trying to make a facsimile of

Lieutenant Chadbourne? Where the real thing won't be found, the only real thing is whatever I make, and I might not do a very good job.)

His letters show his good humor. They show, too, a consistent fairness in his way of reporting. He puts personal limits around what he tells—it's always *his* perspective; not universal truth, not dogma, *just what he has seen or experienced so far.* On August 11, 1839, still in his first week at West Point and just nine days after his seventeenth birthday, he writes to his grandfather, opening his letter with this: "I arrived here on the 5th of this month. As I thought you would like to know how things are managed here, I will try and tell you all I know myself about them." In his letter to George just before his first Christmas at West Point, he tells about "spreeing" and "great doings here" expected on Christmas: "I believe that scarcely a Christmas has passed without somebody's being dismissed for getting drunk or something else. Last year there were several dismissed for throwing coal at some officers who came up to stop the noise in the upper story of North Barracks (alias *Cock-loft*)." He goes on, then, to tell about the death of a cadet:

> Since I began this letter a cadet of the second class has died. He was not much sick when he went down to the hospital, but he grew sicker and in a few days died. They sent after his mother, who lives near Troy, but she got here only to see him die. From what I have heard, I should think his disease was Typhus fever, he seemed to be affected in the same way as another was.

When he writes to his mother from Fort Niagara on November 5, 1843, he tells her about the other officers: "Beside Capt. Morris there are Lieut. McKinstry, Canby and Dr. Mills— From my experience so far it is my opinion that four better men are not to be found in any company in the army." Writing to his father from Toledo, on his way to Texas on September 20, 1845, he says that his trip down Lake Erie has been pleasant and remarks, "The boats on this lake when not too crowded must be the finest and most pleasant to travel in, in the world," but then adds, "I should think though I have not seen the Mississippi boats yet." His November 2, 1845, letter to his father from Corpus Christi reports, "I like what I have seen of my regt. very much." His last letter, dated March 26, 1846, and addressed to his father, tells about the march from Corpus Christi to their present camp nine miles north of Matamoras:

> If I were to begin at the beginning of the march and try to record all the rumors and stories with which we have been perplexed and the orders and movements to which they gave rise, I should not be able to finish my letter in a month. This is emphatically the country of lies and the people have reduced the telling of them to a system which seems to be a part of their religion. Now I don't know whether to tell you first of the country passed over in our march, or to jump at once to the bloody battle we came so near fighting at the crossing of the Colorado. I have no doubt the newspapers will be filled out with lies on the subject. You will understand that at this moment we are 9 miles from the Rio Grande on the Matamoras road, delaying our advance in a very impolitic and unmilitary manner, but as I have a good deal to say on the manner in which the movements of this army have been conducted by the Comd'g General I belive I will wait until we get to Matamoras and see how things finally turn out before I criticize him.

(Listen, literary theorist—you who say the author is not the author but only one in a social community that actually writes the text; you who say that the character of the speaker is not in the text, is only my projection; you who say that the author dies when the reader is born—come and be with me in my life for a while, follow me as I transcribe his letters, watch me wince at the first letters, then shrink at the later letters, then shake at the typewriter as I read his last letters, not as with last letters from a child, but nearly. Of course I never wholly found him. But of course I did, too, and I didn't want him to die. But he died, and I cannot be rid of his presence.)

The one surviving letter that seems to have been consciously composed as a unit is revealing. It is not a small letter: he writes to the adjutant general to say that the president and the army are grievously wrong. We should remember the circumstances of his urgency and outrage. He was a brevet second lieutenant, next in line for promotion to second lieutenant. An opening occurred in the 7th Infantry Regiment, but the commission went to a civilian, Mr. Quimby. Retirement was not mandatory in the army, and most men remained in the service until they died. A promotion could not occur until a vacancy occurred, so a qualified first lieutenant, for example, might wait fifteen years before a place as captain came open in his regiment. The opening, young Chadbourne had thought, was his:

September 9, 1845

Sir:

I have the honor to inform you that I addressed a letter to Headquarters during the latter part of last month, the contents of which related to the appointment by the President of a citizen to fill the vacancy in the Infantry which by regulation belongs to me. After waiting what I suppose a reasonable length of time for an answer, from which I might learn whether or not I can obtain from Headquarters the information sought for concerning the appointment; and it being a matter in which I am very deeply interested, I make this second communication in the hope of learning whether any notice is to be taken of my first one. If I am to expect no answer, I respectfully request that you would inform me of it, as it may make an important difference in the course I shall pursue in relation to the matter in question. I shall more easily overcome the reluctance which I feel in troubling the General in chief by asking for information which I think very probable he may be entirely unable to give; for the reason that the grievance complained of is one affecting in the most serious manner one of the dearest rights of every member of the Army. It would be wasting words to attempt to enlarge upon the consequences of an act which you must of course be so much better able to trace out and appreciate than myself.

I thought (but my inexperience may have led me astray) that my first step should be to lay my complaint officially before the Commander in chief; being at least certain of his disposition to sympathize with even the lowest member of his army, who has suffered an undeserved injury; and his readiness to protect by all means in his power the rights of all under his command. The President has undoubtedly the *power* to deprive me at any moment of the commission which I now hold, without assigning or being able to assign any reason whatever for the act; so he has the power to pursue the course he did in depriving me of the commission which by regulation belonged to me; and were he this day to strike my name from the rolls of the Army, without cause, the second wrong would not be thought by me a greater one than the first, and less easy to be borne without complaint or remonstrance. I believe it my duty, one which I owe to my comrades of my own rank, as well as to myself, to complain of and to resist this act by every means in my power; and if I unfortunately learn that my hopes of promotion are liable to be blasted by a repetition of such acts, I must affirm, and I cannot see

how anyone in the army can differ with me, that any commission
of whatever rank, upon such conditions, is not to be desired.

Very respectfully
I am sir
Your obd't servant

T. L. Chadbourne
Bv't 2nd Lt. 2nd. Infy.

The elegance of his charge is appealing. His first sentence
establishes the occasion and provides a reminder of the first
letter. With a quiet reminder of the delay and of the seriousness of his cause (second sentence), he now requests an answer
(third sentence) one way or another, for that will determine
(fourth sentence) his actions, and there must be action (fifth
sentence) because of the seriousness of the act. While he had
at first thought to write to the president because of his sympathies (sixth sentence), he knows, too (seventh sentence), that
all power rests with the president, which makes his resolve
the stronger (eighth sentence), to show at all costs the consequences of the promotion. His mind runs in interesting ways
here: in the sixth sentence, he refers to the president's pre-
sumed sympathies, but I note that the sympathies appear in
the grammatically subordinate, not the dominant, parts of the
sentence. I note, too, that in the seventh sentence he both states
and shows the president's powers in the first two main clauses,
but the third main clause pits the offense done by power against
power. Finally, I note that in the last sentence, duty and resolve
emerge equated in two major clauses.

There is a courteous, insistent force in the letter—I almost
said a "gentlemanly force." He makes no demands and issues
no threats, but he does want those in authority to know that
what they have done is not trivial or routine, cannot be dismissed as Standard Operational Procedure. He writes *in the
hope* of getting an answer. He knows that there may be no
answer. He knows that the adjutant general can *trace out* the
consequences of the act. He knows his place means doing his
duty with full resolve, which he does, speaking against power
with no trepidation.

As this letter and the passages cited earlier suggest, he had
a wide range of interests and concerns. More: he had a wide
range of capacities, a wide stylistic reach. For example, some

parts of his letters to George, his brother, are joking, boyish
passages, sometimes cryptic in their references to girls. Other
sections of these same letters, however, are full of suggestions
and advice, as in the letter of July 24, 1840: "Be careful who
you get intimate with and mind you don't learn to drink and
smoke. You are not likely to have more temptation than I have
had. Stick to your place and go *ahead straight* for your own
sake and for that of all of us. Try and write often and we will
do each other all the good we can." In his letter of February 13,
1842, in which he earlier chides George for not filling up the
page when he writes, this advice appears:

> also read every book you can get hold of. That will inform your
> mind and taste: don't waste time on the common miserable trashy
> novels so plenty everywhere. They are worse than useless. In short
> you should study to improve yourself now while there is time and
> opportunity; and George we both need it enough in all conscience.

He was also solicitous of his father, though in different ways.
Writing on May 9, 1843, as graduation nears, he apologizes for
the brevity of his letter: "I hate to break off this letter on the
second page, but my ideas and time are both exhausted and
these few lines will serve to assure you of my safety and good
health." In his last letter, March 26, 1846, also to his father,
this appears:

> We have defied them by playing Yankee Doodle and hoisting our
> flag under their very noses. Now if they choose to attempt to drive
> us away, let them try it and we shall see. I should like very well
> to get into Matamoras it looks quite well from here and I have a
> great desire to live in some sort of a house once more. I suppose the
> newspapers will be full of false accounts of anything that may or
> has transpired, so don't make yourself uneasy at anything you may
> see, and if any length of time should elapse without your hearing
> from me directly be sure that nothing happened worth telling of.

The nature of his care is indicated, too, in his comments
about his aunt Mary. Earlier, he had invited her to come to
see him and to watch him command the guard, but then he
learned that she was deathly ill and wrote to George:

> I cannot bear to think that Aunt Mary is about to be taken away
> from us, but I suppose we have no good ground to expect her re-
> covery: what a lovely woman she is, George—she has been more a

sister to us than Aunt: we shall not "look upon her like again"—
It will be painful to go home and see her die, but it would be still
more so were I never to see her again. From all I can hear, it seems
her spirits keep up wonderfully. Is she able to go about house at all
now? What a blow it will be to Grandmother.

Evidence of the manner in which he treated his mother is, I
think, particularly revealing. Link Chadbourne was the oldest
of nine children. One of his younger brothers, Nedd, died in
the fall of 1839, after Link had gone to West Point. In the spring
of 1841 he received word of the birth of Thomas, who was to
be the last child. Link had still not been home: cadets were not
allowed to leave until the summer following their second year.
He opens his letter to his mother, May 12, 1841, acknowledging the birth: "I have rec. your last letter informing me that
there is somebody at home whom I never saw. There are just as
many of us now as there were when I went away, he will take
Nedd's place with me." Otherwise, he often teases his mother,
especially about the last child, Tom, and about how deplor-
ably lax she has become in bringing the boy up. The boots he
refers to are apparently some that he brought home as a gift
for the little boy. When he refers to his own boots, he is talking
about some that his father ordered for him during his first year
at West Point. He writes to his mother on November 5, 1843,
from Fort Niagara:

> Here I am all alone by myself (but one might have worse company
> though)—my room is a sort of sanctum sanctorum which visitors
> never disturb. However I have scarce ever felt lonely in it—when-
> ever I perceive any such feeling is coming on I drive it off by consid-
> ering that if you were all here, I should be pestered with that little
> ridiculous plague of a Tom and there are cross young ones enough
> here now—That young gent will certainly be the scapegrace of the
> family—I doubt whether you will be able to whip him when he is
> in his boots. Now this of itself is enough to ruin him for he needs
> at least six whippings a day, Sundays more. He will be just as many
> times worse a character than myself as the number of years differ-
> ence in the age at which we respectively became possessed of a pair
> of the above mentioned articles. Now the difference is somewhere
> about fifteen years. This is all evident enough from the fact that I
> am decidedly the best of your children, why, partly because I waited
> longest for my boots. Indian pudding, Mother, is a thing I despair
> of seeing unless I do make it myself.

And, I believe, he shows me another trait in his letters, a kind

of directness, an unflinching honesty in the way he faced life.
Shortly after arriving at Fort Niagara, he writes to his father
on October 3, 1843: "Sunday having nothing else to do I took a
wagon and rode up to the falls—There is nothing left for common persons to tell about them, all we can do, is to enjoy them
and say not a word." In this respect, what he remembers is an
index. On August 13, 1845, still caught up in the quarrel about
his promotion but also expecting soon to go to Texas, he writes
to his father:

> What a jolly time we will have in Texas, four or five regts together,
> cruising about on the prairies. I now think (and in fact have often
> thought since she said it) of what Grandmother said when you first
> talked of sending me to West Point. Somebody remarked to her in
> my hearing that if I went there I should probably be sent off to the
> west to fight Indians the rest of my days and perhaps be scalped
> by them. She answered, Well, why not he, as well as any one else,
> somebody must run the risk, and if it's right for one to do it, it is for
> another. I never forgot that remark. It is characteristic of Grand-
> mother it shows her spirit. She never felt that anyone belonging
> to her was too good to be employed in any necessary and proper
> service however laborious or dangerous it might be.

But its revelation of an unflinching look at life makes a later
passage leap off the page. On November 2, 1845, having arrived at Corpus Christi, he writes to tell his father about his
trip. His letter includes a graphic account of a fatal accident as
they were landing. A steamboat had come alongside to help in
the unloading. Its topmast caught in his vessel's rigging, broke
off, and fell, striking a young officer named Merrill, who had
only that summer graduated from West Point:

> He died about 3½ hours after the accident and we buried him next
> day. It was an awfully sudden thing, and we felt that it might have
> been any one of us as well as him. Poor fellow! he never knew what
> hurt him. But his parents! I hope if I die a violent death it may be
> in a way that will do some good either real or pretended.

In the letters that survive, I found no trace of deceit or rancor.
He is never merely self-serving, never mean-spirited. He is a
gentle, funny, honest, strong young man, with a wide-ranging
capacity for care.

And he slips away from me. Why wouldn't he? I can't remember who *I* was five years ago, let alone the whom somebody else remembers from five years ago. He slips away from me, and doesn't. What of the other letters, I wonder, those I didn't see? What of himself, whom I didn't see, and did?

Eighteen

A Last Question

I have come to the chapter that I can't write. I don't know what I need to know.

I wanted to know who recommended that the fort be named for him. Who recommended the name? There were, of course, corollary questions: When was Link Chadbourne's name recommended? Where was it recommended? Who was thinking of him, remembering him, and why?

General Order 11, dated February 6, 1852, declares that "all new posts which may be hereafter established, will receive their names from the War Department, and be announced in General Orders from the Head Quarters of the Army." However official, that wasn't always the case. As Robert W. Frazier observes in *Forts of the West*, "the sources for the names of forts continued to vary. Some posts were named by the officers who established them, others by the officers who ordered their establishment, still others by the general in command of the army, and some by the secretary of war." One hundred and seventy-one forts west of the Mississippi were named for officers—1 for a general of the army, 17 for major generals, 31 for brigadier generals, 40 for colonels, 11 for lieutenant colonels, 15 for majors, 36 for captains, 13 for first lieutenants, 6 for second lieutenants, and 1 for a brevet second lieutenant.

In the instance of Fort Chadbourne, it was Special Order 46, October 25, 1852. Headquarters, 8th Department, had already declared what the name would be. Had someone recommended

Lieutenant Chadbourne's name earlier? Was someone just
going down a list of recently fallen officers? Was it a ceremo-
nial, not a personal, decision?

The post returns for Fort Chadbourne were written too late
to tell much. It was established in October 1852 by Captain
John Beardsley (West Point, 1841), commanding companies
A and K of the 8th Infantry Regiment and the only officer
present excepting the surgeon. I expect that Captain Beardsley
knew Link Chadbourne—he was a second lieutenant in the
8th Infantry at Resaca de la Palma.

But there was that other post, temporarily named Camp
Chadbourne, near Fredericksburg and later called Fort Martin
Scott. A post return for Camp Chadbourne exists for April
1849. The commanding officer there was Captain W. R. Montgomery (West Point, 1825), who was also at Resaca de la Palma.
Three West Pointers were among the other seven officers assigned to the post—Collinson R. Gates (class of 1836), Alfred
St. Amand Crozet (class of 1843), and James Snelling (class
of 1845). All were also with the 8th Infantry during the Mexican War.

Who was remembering Link Chadbourne? Who kept his
name?

The information is there somewhere, I expect, but I haven't
found it.

Nineteen

Perhaps I'll Never
Find Him

He slips away from me, and why wouldn't he? I can't re-member who *I* was five years ago, let alone the whom someone else remembers from five years ago. He slips away from me, and doesn't. What of the other letters, I wonder, those I didn't see? What of himself, whom I didn't see, and did?

Was there a piano, I wonder, in the theater the officers built in Corpus Christi, and did he play for the musical perfor-mances?

And what of the letters I didn't read,—those, I guess, that didn't survive? Is he there rather than here? Have I caught glimpses of him, glimpses?

I'm not sure that *I'm* willing to be altogether here at the behest of whoever drops by to read.

What of the letters I didn't read? Is he there rather than here?

And what of the others?

What of all those whose names I didn't keep and celebrate, counted but didn't record, back in chapter 6; all those young men who died, about a third of the 856 who were graduated in the classes from 1842 through 1861. They died in strange places, and I didn't keep their names; perhaps at home, or at Tampico, Mexico City, in Texas at Fort Terrett, in a steam-ship wreck in Long Island Sound, in New Mexico against the Apaches, in Florida or California, in Texas, drowned in

the Rio Grande, at Resaca de la Palma, Contreras, Monter-
rey, at sea, at Bull Run, Molino del Rey, Chapultepec, the
Wilderness, Fort Washita, Fort Steilacoom, in Cuba, at Chan-
cellorsville, Fort Tejon, in Utah, at Churubusco, Camargo, Fort
Gibson, Fort McKavett, Fort Independence, Fort Monroe, in
Kentucky, Tennessee, Washington Territory, at Fort Randall,
Fort Bliss, Fort Yuma, in Virginia, at Fort Brown, Gettysburg,
Chickamauga, Fort Craig, Valverde, Spottsylvania, in Nicaragua, at Antietam, in Peru, at Fort Laramie, Fort Reno, Shiloh,
Fort Moultrie, Fort Leavenworth, in Texas against the Comanches, at Gaines Mill, Fredericksburg, Fort Clark, Cold Har-
bor, in the Dakotas, elsewhere, elsewhere. In his *Mexican War
Diary*, George B. McClellan, class of 1846, tells about being
sick when he arrived at Matamoros and later on his way to Camargo. He tells about his quarters there, shared with Jimmie
Stuart, who "came down to take care of me when I first got
there, and after doing so with his usual kindness was unfortunately taken with a fever, and had to stay there anyhow." A
footnote adds this:

> Later on McClellan wrote in the diary on a page otherwise blank:
> "On the 18th June, 1851, at five in the afternoon died Jimmie
> Stuart, my best and oldest friend. He was mortally wounded the day
> before by an arrow, whilst gallantly leading a charge against a party
> of hostile Indians. He is buried at Camp Stuart—about twenty-five
> miles south of Rogue's River [Oregon?], near the main road, and
> not far from the base of the Cichion (?) Mountains. His grave is
> between two oaks, on the left side of the road, going south, with
> J. S. cut in the bark of the largest of the oaks."

This is James Stuart, class of 1846, born in South Carolina.
They died in strange places.

And what of William Hunter Churchill, class of 1840, son of
General Sylvanus Churchill and perhaps the boyhood friend
of Link Chadbourne, dead in Texas in 1847?

And what of Henry McKavett, class of 1834, captain, 8th Infantry Regiment, who fought at Resaca de la Palma and was
killed at Monterrey? Raised in the New York Orphan Asylum,
he left most of his property to that institution upon his death.
M. L. Crimmins reports that at Resaca de la Palma he dis-
played great coolness and judgment, and "distinguished him-

self in leading his company into action, in the brilliant charge made by Colonel Belknap. He fell at Monterey, at the head of his company, under peculiarly affecting circumstances, a cannon ball literally severing him in twain."

And what of Captain D. José Barragan? In *The Other Side*, translated and edited by Albert C. Ramsey, Ramón Alcaraz reports from the other side:

> The enemy, in the meanwhile, attacked the 2d Light, which was weak from being employed in the advance guard. In it was found a strong resistance, as well as in the companies of the sharpshooters, the 4th and the 6th, commanded by the gallant Captains D. José Barragan and D. José María Moreno. The 2d Light fought with decided courage. The two heroic companies did battle with a great part of the North American army. Their extraordinary efforts of valor shone brightly against the immense numerial superiority of their opponents. Barragan fell mortally wounded . . .

And what of Captain Arana of the Tampico Guards? He died, Alcaraz reports, "like a brave man."

And what of Lieutenant R. E. Cochran, not of West Point, 4th Infantry Regiment, dead on the field at Resaca de la Palma? He made it through the resaca and went on beyond with troops to overrun General Arista's headquarters. He was killed there.

And what of Zebulon Montgomery Pike Inge of Alabama, class of 1838, first lieutenant, dragoons, dead on the field at Resaca de la Palma? Thorpe reports that "during Capt. May's charge, Lieut. Z. M. P. Inge fell at the head of his platoon, mortally wounded in the throat by a cannon shot; his horse was also killed. In the midst of the battle, his body was stripped by the rancheros, and mutilated with their spears."

And what of Theodore Lincoln Chadbourne of Eastport, Maine, second lieutenant, 8th Infantry Regiment, killed at Resaca de la Palma, May 9, 1846? What of Link Chadbourne?

Notes on Sources

Sources adequately identified in the text are not listed here. Other bibliographical resources are listed below by chapter, generally in the order in which I have used them.

Chapter 2

I've depended here on Rupert Richardson's *The Frontier of Northwest Texas* (Glendale, Calif.: A. H. Clark, 1963).

Chapter 3

Here, I refer to Ray Miller, *Texas Forts* (Houston: Cordovan Press, 1985); and *Eyes of Texas Travel Guide*, Hill Country/Permian Basin Edition (Houston, Cordovan Press, 1980); Charles M. Robinson, *Frontier Forts of Texas* (Houston: Lone Star Books, n.d.); and Jessie Newton Yarbrough, *A History of Coke County* (Privately printed, 1979).

Chapter 4

In addition to a couple of items identified in the text, I have relied on the following: Joel Conarroe, "This Boy's Life," *New York Times Book Review*, January 15, 1989; Samuel Hynes, "In the Whirl and Muddle of War," *New York Times Book Review*, July 31, 1988; Annie Dillard, *An American Childhood* (New York: Harper and Row, 1987); Israel Rosenfield, "Neural Darwinism: A New Approach to Memory and Perception," *New York Review of Books*, October 9, 1986; Claire Tomalin, "Frankenstein's Mother," *New York Review of Books*, November 19, 1987; Bruce Duffy, "The Do-It-Yourself Life of Ludwig

Wittgenstein," *New York Times Book Review*, November 13, 1980; Studs Terkel, *The Good War* (New York: Pantheon, 1984); Martin Filler, "Looking for Mr. Wright," *New York Times Book Review*, December 13, 1987; Shirley Hazzard, "Chaos Was His Opportunity," *New York Times Book Review*, March 27, 1988; and Louis Simpson, *Selected Prose* (New York: Paragon House, 1989).

Chapter 6

I cite Evan Connell, *Son of the Morning Star* (San Francisco: North Point Press, 1984).

Chapter 10

I refer to Robert W. Frazier, *Forts of the West* (Norman: University of Oklahoma Press, 1972).

Chapter 11

I refer to Stanley Fish, *Is There a Text In This Class?* (Cambridge, Mass.: Harvard University Press, 1980); and to Roland Barthes, *Image, Music, Text* (New York: Hill and Wang, 1977).

Chapter 12

I refer to David C. Hensley's *Brigadier General Sylvester Churchill* (Fallon, Nev.: Western American History Series, 1988); and I've relied throughout on the following: *The Centennial of the United States Military Academy at West Point, New York*, 2 vols. (Washington, D.C.: Government Printing Office, 1904); J. H. Colton, *A Guide Book to West Point and Vicinity; Containing Descriptive, Historical, and Statistical Sketches of the United States Military Academy, and of Other Objects of Interest* (New York: J. H. Colton, 1844); Joseph B. James, "Life at West Point One Hundred Years Ago," *Mississippi Valley Historical Review* (June 1944); James L. Morrison, *The Best School in the World* (Kent, Ohio: Kent State University Press, 1986); and Stephen E. Ambrose, *Duty, Honor, Country* (Baltimore: Johns Hopkins University Press, 1966).

Chapter 14

In addition to newspapers and other sources that are sufficiently identified in the text, I have relied on the following for accounts of troop movements and of the battle of Resaca de la Palma: Ulysses S.

Grant, *Papers* (Carbondale: Southern Illinois University Press, 1967);
W. S. Henry, *Campaign Sketches of the War with Mexico* (New York:
Arno Press, 1973); Samuel French, *Two Wars* (Nashville: Confederate Veterans, 1901); George Meade, *Life and Letters* (New York:
Charles Scribner's Sons, 1913); Ethan Allan Hitchcock, *Fifty Years
in Camp and Field* (New York: G. P. Putnam's Sons, 1909); James
Longstreet, *From Manassas to Appomattox* (Bloomington: Indiana
University Press, 1896); George Winston Smith and Charles Judah,
Chronicles of the Gringos (Albuquerque: University of New Mexico
Press, 1968); Oliver Spaulding, *The United States Army in War and
Peace* (New York: G. P. Putnam's Sons, 1937); Alfred H. Bill, *Rehearsal
for Conflict* (New York: Alfred A. Knopf, 1947); Seymour Connor and
Odie B. Faulk, *North America Divided* (New York: Oxford University Press, 1971); David Lavender, *Climax at Buena Vista* (Philadelphia: Lippincott, 1966); John S. D. Eisenhower, *So Far from God*
(New York: Random House, 1989); Edward Nichols, *Zach Taylor's
Little Army* (New York: Doubleday, 1963); J. E. Weems, *To Conquer a
Peace* (Garden City, N.Y.: Doubleday, 1974); Justin Smith, *The War
with Mexico* (New York: Macmillan, 1919); N. C. Brooks, *A Complete
History of the War with Mexico* (Philadelphia: Griggs, Elliot, 1849);
Ronnie Tyler, *The Mexican War, a Lithographic Record* (Austin: Texas
State Historical Association, 1973); Joseph Sides, *Fort Brown Historical* (San Antonio: Naylor, 1942); Zachary Taylor, *Letters from the
Battle-fields of the Mexican War* (New York: Klaus Reprint Company,
1970); Charles J. Peterson, *The Military Heroes of the War with Mexico*
(Philadelphia: Leary, 1848); Theophilus Rodenbaugh and William
Haskin, *The Army of the United States* (New York: Maynard, Merrill, 1896); Isaac Stevens, *Campaigns of the Rio Grande and of Mexico*
(New York: D. Appleton, 1851); Lloyd Lewis, *Captain Sam Grant*
(Boston: Little, Brown, 1950); Freeman Cleaves, *Meade of Gettysburg*
(Norman: University of Oklahoma Press, 1959); Emma Jerome Blackwood, *To Mexico with Scott, Letters of Captain E. Kirby Smith and
His Wife* (Cambridge, Mass.: Harvard University Press, 1917); Roswell
Ripley, *The War with Mexico* (New York: Harper, 1849); Rhoda Van
Bibber Tanner Doubleday, *Journals of the Late Brevet Major Philip
Norbourne Barbour and His Wife Isabella Hopkins Barbour* (New
York: G. P. Putnam's Sons, 1936); Thomas Wilhelm, *History of the
8th U.S. Infantry* (Headquarters 8th Infantry, 1873); Robert Johannsen, *To the Halls of the Montezumas* (New York: Oxford University
Press, 1985); Hal Bridges, *Lee's Maverick General, Daniel Harvey Hill*
(New York: McGraw-Hill, 1961); Horatio Ladd, *History of the War
with Mexico* (New York: Dodd, Mead, 1883); Charles L. Dufour, *The*

Mexican War, A Compact History, 1846–1848 (New York: Hawthorn
Books, 1968); John Frost, *The Mexican War and Its Warriors* (New
Haven: Mansfield, 1859); John Frost, *Pictorial History of Mexico and
the Mexican War* (Philadelphia: Thomas Cowperthwaite, 1848); John
Jenkins, *History of the War Between the United States and Mexico*
(Auburn, Ala.: Derby and Miller, 1851); Cadmus Wilcox, *History of
the Mexican War* (Washington, D.C.: Church News Publishing Com-
pany, 1892); Editors of Time-Life, *The Mexican War* (Alexandria,
Va.: Time-Life Books, 1978); John Sedgwick, *Correspondence* (New
York: Battel, 1903); H. H. Bancroft, *History of Mexico*, vol. 5 (New
York: McGraw-Hill, 1885); T. B. Thorpe, *Our Army on the Rio Grande*
(Philadelphia: Carey and Hart, 1846); and G. W. Kendall, *The War
Between the United States and Mexico* (New York: D. Appleton, 1851).

Chapter 15

I've continued to depend here on many of the sources just cited above.
I also cite James Warner Bellah, *The Apache* (New York: Gold Medal
Books, 1951).

After completing most of the work for this book, I came upon *Monterrey Is Ours! The Mexican War Letters of Lieutenant Dana*, edited
by Robert H. Ferrell (Lexington: University Press of Kentucky, 1990),
and was again struck by a quality in reporting that I do not altogether
understand—perhaps a sense of professionalism or of military deco-
rum or protocol. Lieutenant Napoleon Jackson Tecumseh Dana was
born in Eastport, Maine, too, only months before Link Chadbourne.
They surely knew each other. Dana entered West Point in 1838, a
year ahead of Chadbourne, and graduated in 1842; they were there
together for three years. Even so, Lieutenant Dana's letter of May 13,
1846, in which he tells of the battle at Resaca de la Palma, notes
only that Lieutenant Chadbourne was among those killed. Otherwise,
silence again.

Chapter 16

Most of the sources I depend upon here have already been identified in the notes for chapter 3 above. I should add Joe Gibson, *Forts
and Treasure Trails of West Texas* (San Angelo, Tex.: Educators Press,
1969); Herbert M. Hart, *Old Forts of the Southwest* (Seattle: Superior
Publishing Company, 1964); and Averam Bender, *The March of Empire* (New York: Greenwood Press, 1968).

I use George B. McClellan, *The Mexican War Diary* (Princeton: Princeton University Press, 1917); and Albert C. Ramsey's contemporary translation of *The Other Side; or, Notes for the History of the War Between Mexico and the United States* (Originally published in Mexico in 1848. Reprint. New York: B. Franklin, 1970).